EDITOR'S LETTER

Border control

Borders have never been more porous than today for authoritarians, and we should all be afraid, writes **JEMIMAH STEINFELD**

IMAGINE ONE OF those spot the difference-style picture games you did as a child. The left image is of Sun Yat-sen, a Chinese dissident, being dragged into London's Chinese Embassy in 1896; the right is of another Chinese dissident being dragged into the Chinese consulate in Manchester in 2022. Superficially it looks like not much has changed, beyond presumably more modern clothes and the location. Both are examples, after all, of what has come to be somewhat clunkily termed "transnational repression" – when states reach beyond their borders to silence opposition, in these instances very physically yanking people into Chinese government buildings in the UK.

Except in the first instance you have the most high-profile Chinese dissident of the age, a man who went onto become president of the Republic of China, while the recent example is someone who was referred to as "unknown man" in media reports from the time. And this is arguably the biggest difference, even if it's not apparent to the naked eye; today the dividing line between who is and who isn't a target of autocratic regimes abroad has faded so much that it pretty much includes anyone – you and me – who doesn't internalise their criticisms.

This is the reality of the world we live in. Last century dissidents could and did flee countries of persecution to seek a new, safe life elsewhere, and we too could criticise states from afar without fear that our words would come back to haunt us. Gone are those days. Changing geopolitical ties, more belligerent leaders and vast improvements to the technological landscape have created a toxic potion, one that has essentially eroded the sanctity once provided by the border.

We explore this in our first issue of 2024. We ask what has changed, starting with a thoughtful essay from the academic Alexander Dukalskis on the history of transnational repression and moving onto a compare and contrast with Zhou Fengsuo, a Tiananmen Square leader who fled China for the USA in the 1990s, and Nathan Law, the face of Hong Kong's pro-democracy movement who has lived in the UK since 2020. Russian dissidents write for us about their very real fear for their lives. The Salisbury attacks on Sergei and Yulia Skripal sent a message: even your doorknobs can be smeared with poison.

Sitting alongside these articles are examples of less physically confronting ways critics are being silenced overseas. Belarusian activist Hanna Komar has run out of passport pages and is unable to renew unless she goes back to Belarus. She can't. She'd be instantly arrested. Komar joins dissidents from Iran and Qatar whose passports are being held to ransom, while India is denying entry visas to anyone who is critical of Narendra Modi.

The articles are underlined by a concern that the frog is truly in boiling water. Yes, we are talking about transnational repression more than before and yet we're not taking action. Victories happen, such as the Saudi comedian who has successfully sued Saudi Arabia for spyware on his phone. And yet these victories are small and only treat the symptom not the cause. We need a more unified approach. Consider this issue a sounding horn. ✖

Jemimah Steinfeld, editor-in-chief

53(01):1/1|DOI:10.1177/03064220241243207

Long arms are getting longer

Our cover artists on escaping a Hong Kong being carved in Beijing's image only to still fear Beijing's touch

Long-Armed People, oil on canvas, is a co-created work by artists Lumli Lumlong who were forced to leave their home in Hong Kong for the UK in 2021.

The left side is painted by husband, Lumlong, and the right is painted by wife, Lumli.

The artists said of the work: "When you think you've left your homeland and escaped it, it reappears. When you believe you're sitting safely at home, it's watching you. When transnational repression has penetrated deep into your bones, your only option is to overcome fear and rise to resist it."

Their artwork typically exposes social realities and has been exhibited, and collected, around the world. For them reality is more scary than their art and compassion is central in fighting repression.

INDEX ON CENSORSHIP | VOL.53 | NO.1

CONTENTS

Up Front

1 **BORDER CONTROL:**
   JEMIMAH STEINFELD
   There's no safe place for the world's dissidents. World leaders need to act

6 **THE INDEX: MARK FRARY**
   A glimpse at the world of free expression, featuring Indian elections, Predator spyware and a Bahraini hunger strike

Features

14 **JUST PASSING THROUGH:**
   EDUARDO HALFON
   A guided tour through Guatemala's crime traps

17 **EXPORTING THE AMERICAN PLAYBOOK: AMY FALLON**
   The culture wars are finding new ground in Canada, where the freedom to read is the latest battle

20 **THE COUPLE AND THE KING:**
   CLEMENCE MANYUKWE
   Tanele Maseko saw her activist husband killed in front of her eyes, but it has not stopped her fight for democracy

23 **OBRADOR'S PARTING GIFT:**
   CHRIS HAVLER-BARRETT
   Journalists are free to report in Mexico, as long as it's what the president wants to hear

26 **SILENCING THE FAITHFUL:**
   SIMONE DIAS MARQUES
   Brazil's religious minorities are under attack

28 **THE ANTI-ABORTION ROADSHOW: REBECCA L ROOT**
   The USA's most controversial new export could be a campaign against reproductive rights

32 **THE WOMAN TAKING ON THE TROLLS: DAISY RUDDOCK**

UP FRONT

Tackling disinformation has left Marianna Spring a victim of trolling, even by Elon Musk

34 BROKEN NEWS: MEHRAN FIRDOUS
The founder of The Kashmir Walla reels from his time in prison and the banning of his news outlet

38 WHO CAN WE TRUST?: KIMBERLEY BROWN
Organised crime and corruption have turned once peaceful Ecuador into a reporter's nightmare

41 THE COST OF BEING GREEN: THIÊN VIÊT
Vietnam's environmental activists are mysteriously all being locked up on tax charges

44 WHO IS THE REAL ENEMY?: RAPHAEL RASHID
Where North Korea is concerned, poetry can go too far — according to South Korea

47 THE LAW, WHEN IT SUITS HIM: JP O'MALLEY
Donald Trump could be making prison cells great again

Special Report: The long reach

52 NOWHERE IS SAFE: ALEXANDER DUKALSKIS
Introducing the new and improved ways that autocracies silence their overseas critics

54 WELCOME TO THE DICTATORS' PLAYGROUND: KAYA GENÇ
When it comes to safeguarding immigrant dissidents, Turkey has a bad reputation

58 THE OVERSEAS REPRESSORS WHO ARE EVADING THE SPOTLIGHT: EMILY COUCH
It's not all Russia, China and Saudi Arabia. Central Asian governments are reaching across borders too

61 EVERYTHING EVERYWHERE ALL AT ONCE: DAISY RUDDOCK
It's both quantity and quality when it comes to how states attack dissent abroad

62 A FATAL GAME OF INTERNATIONAL HIDE AND SEEK: DANSON KAHYANA
After leaving Eritrea, one writer lives in constant fear of being kidnapped or killed

64 OUR PRINCIPLES ARE NOT FOR SALE: JIRAPREEYA SAEBOO
The Thai student publisher who told China to keep their cash bribe

66 REFUSED A PASSPORT: SALLY GIMSON
A lesson from Belarus in how to obstruct your critics

69 BE NICE, OR YOU'RE NOT COMING IN: SALIL TRIPATHI
Is the murder of a Sikh activist in Canada the latest in India's cross-border control?

74 AN AGENCY FOR THOSE DENIED AGENCY: AMY FALLON
The Sikh Press Association's members are no strangers to receiving death threats

75 ALWAYS LOOKING BEHIND: ZHOU FENGSUO, NATHAN LAW
If you're a Tiananmen protest leader or the face of Hong Kong's democracy movement, China is always watching

78 PUTTING INTERPOL ON NOTICE: TOMMY GREENE
For dissidents who find themselves on Red Notice, it's all about location, location, location

80 LIVING IN RUSSIA'S SHADOW: IRINA BABLOYAN, ANDREI SOLDATOV, KIRILL MARTYNOV
Three Russian journalists in exile outline why paranoia around their safety is justified

Comment

86 SOLIDARITY, ASSANGE-STYLE: MARTIN BRIGHT
Our editor-at-large on his own experience working with Assange

88 CHALLENGING WORDS: EMMA L BRIANT
An academic on what to do around the weaponisation of words

90 GOOD, BAD AND EVERYTHING THAT'S IN BETWEEN: RUTH ANDERSON
New threats to free speech call for new approaches

Culture

94 UKRAINE'S DISAPPEARING INK: VICTORIA AMELINA, STEPHEN KOMARNYCKYJ
One of several Ukrainian writers killed in Russia's war, Amelina's words live on

101 ONE-WAY TICKET TO FREEDOM?: GHANEM AL MASARIR, JEMIMAH STEINFELD
A dissident has the last laugh on Saudi, when we publish his skit

104 THE SHOW MUST GO ON: KATIE DANCEY-DOWNS, YAHYA MAREI, BAHAA ELDIN IBDAH
In the midst of war Palestine's Freedom Theatre still deliver cultural resistance, some of which is published here

110 FIGHT FOR LIFE – AND LANGUAGE: WILLIAM YANG
Uyghur linguists are doing everything they can to keep their culture alive

112 FREEDOM IS VERY FRAGILE: MARK FRARY, OLEKSANDRA MATVIICHUK
The winner of the 2022 Nobel Peace Prize on looking beyond the Nuremberg Trials lens

INDEXONCENSORSHIP.ORG

CHIEF EXECUTIVE
Ruth Anderson
EDITOR-IN-CHIEF
Jemimah Steinfeld
ASSISTANT EDITOR
Katie Dancey-Downs
EDITOR-AT-LARGE
Martin Bright
ASSOCIATE EDITOR
Mark Frary
ART DIRECTOR
Matthew Hasteley
EDITORIAL ASSISTANT
Daisy Ruddock
SUB EDITORS
Adam Aiken, Tracey Bagshaw, Jan Fox, Sally Gimson
CONTRIBUTING EDITORS
Kaya Genç, Emily Couch, Danson Kahyana, Salil Tripathi
HEAD OF POLICY & CAMPAIGNS
Jessica Ní Mhainín
POLICY & CAMPAIGNS OFFICER
Nik Williams
DEVELOPMENT OFFICER - FUNDRAISING & EVENTS
Anna Millward
DIRECTORS & TRUSTEES
Trevor Phillips (Chair), Kate Maltby (Vice Chair), Anthony Barling, Andrew Franklin, James Goode, Helen Mountfield, Elaine Potter, Mark Stephens, Nick Timothy, Ian Rosenblatt
PATRONS
Margaret Atwood, Simon Callow, Steve Coogan, Brian Eno, Christopher Hird, Jude Kelly, Michael Palin, Matthew Parris, Alexandra Pringle, Gabrielle Rifkind, Sir Tom Stoppard, Lady Sue Woodford Hollick
ADVISORY COMMITTEE
Julian Baggini, Jeff Wasserstrom, Emma Briant, Ariel Dorfman, Michael Foley, Conor Gearty, AC Grayling, Lyndsay Griffiths, William Horsley, Anthony Hudson, Natalia Koliada, Jane Kramer, Jean-Paul Marthoz, Robert McCrum, Rebecca MacKinnon, Beatrice Mtetwa, Julian Petley, Michael Scammell, Kamila Shamsie, Michael Smyth, Tess Woodcraft, Christie Watson

The Index

A round-up of events in the world of free expression from Index's unparalleled network of writers and activists

Edited by
MARK FRARY

53(01):6/10|DOI:10.1177/03064220241243208

PICTURED: Police officers violently restrain a man during a gathering in memory of opposition leader Alexei Navalny near Moscow's Wall of Grief, following his death at the Polar Wolf penal colony on 16 February

The Index

ELECTION WATCH

The bumper election year has started. Here's who is heading to the polls next

LEFT TO RIGHT: Outgoing Mexican President Obrador; India's Modi; Mauritania President Ghazouani

1. India

APRIL/MAY 2024

The Indian general election is a major event staggered across April and May, taking weeks to come to a conclusion. India says this is due to security, which is necessary to protect the integrity of the election. However, it would be a stretch to say that elections in the state are free and fair.

It is widely expected that current Prime Minister Narendra Modi will be elected for a third term. His party, the Bharatiya Janata party (BJP), particularly appeals to the Hindu majority in the country amidst rising attacks on Muslims. There are serious concerns about freedoms in the country under Modi, who has been accused of targeting political opponents such as opposition candidates, rights activists and academics in order to silence dissenters. Critics warn that media freedom and judicial independence have also suffered during Modi's reign, which looks set to be extended this summer.

2. Mexico

2 JUNE 2024

Mexico's last general election, which took place in 2018 and saw the appointment of Andres Manuel Lopez Obrador (Amlo) as the country's president, was marred by violence as criminal organisations used targeted violence to secure their own political interests. Candidates for office were threatened, there were allegations of widespread illicit campaign activities and at least 145 people died as a result of election-related violence. The midterm elections in 2021 saw a similar upturn in violence, with at least 34 electoral candidates murdered and hundreds more threatened or attacked according to Mexican authorities. The June election is of huge importance; the country is electing not only a new head of state, which cannot be Amlo due to constitutional rules limiting presidents to one term only, but all legislators at both national and state level. If this pattern of violence continues the impact will be felt across the entire political system, which puts democracy at risk.

3. Mauritania

22 JUNE 2024

Mauritania is due to hold its presidential election in June as President Mohamed Ould Cheikh Ghazouani's first five-year term comes to an end. The country's constitution allows the president to serve two terms, meaning Ghazouani will be vying for re-election. Ghazouani took over the presidency from former political ally Mohamed Ould Abdel Aziz, who himself came into power following a military coup in 2008.

The country has gradually become more open and has conducted peaceful transfers of power since, but elections are flawed and the executive remains dominant. The Mauritanian government has been known to restrict opposition both politically and in the media, such as when reporter Abdellahi Mohamed Ould Atigha was arrested for a Facebook post questioning government spending, so although improvements have been made concerns remain over the openness of the upcoming election. ✖

MY INSPIRATION

Rights are taken not given

Bahraini dissident **SAYED ALWADAEI** talks about **DR ABDULJALIL AL-SINGACE** who shows how difficult it is to break someone's soul

I HAD HEARD his name before I ever met him, and getting to know him personally has been an honour and continued source of inspiration for me. Now 62 years old and a symbol for the broader struggle for freedom and democracy in Bahrain, he has shown that it is indeed difficult to break someone's soul.

His name is Dr Abduljalil Al-Singace, an award-winning human rights defender serving a life sentence in Bahrain for his role in the mass pro-democracy protests in Bahrain's capital Manama during the 2011 Arab Spring.

Born with polio, Al-Singace has had to rely on crutches, but his disability did not prevent him from getting a PhD in impact mechanics, going on to head Bahrain University's Department of Mechanical Engineering and becoming one of the most distinguished academics in the country.

Dr Abduljalil Al-Singace holds many titles — human rights defender, activist, author, academic, engineer, blogger, professor, father, husband — but a quitter he is not and his resilience and determination is beyond belief.

Soon he will complete 1,000 days without solid food. He has been on hunger strike since 7 July 2021 to protest the confiscation of his research manuscripts in the form of handwritten notes which he spent four years writing, relying only on limited resources in the prison. He wrote about different Bahraini dialects and colloquial sayings that have rolled from one generation to the next. He will not end his hunger strike until the Bahraini Government restores his rights and transfers his confiscated research to his family.

His ongoing suffering mirrors the experiences of many Bahrainis who have been struggling for political reform in the country. But his resilience in the face of persecution serves as inspiration for us to continue the fight.

He has often said that "rights are taken, not given" and that "Change, democracy, dreams […] Things that don't come easily to us"— Dr Al-Singace is an embodiment of a difficult, brave and unwavering fight for justice and freedom. ✖

> His ongoing suffering mirrors the experiences of many Bahrainis who have been struggling for political reform

Free speech in numbers

47

The age at which Putin critic Alexei Navalny died in an Arctic penal colony of reported "sudden death syndrome"

10

Number of years jail term that could be faced by anyone involved in LGBTQ+ campaigns aimed at children under new laws passed in Ghana in February

200,000

The amount in dollars reportedly offered to a people smuggler by Iranian spies to assassinate two Persian-language Iran International reporters in London. The plot was foiled

94

Journalists and media workers confirmed dead since 7 October in Gaza

89

Journalists and media workers confirmed dead since 7 October in Gaza who are Palestinian

The Index

PEOPLE WATCH

DAISY RUDDOCK highlights the stories of human rights defenders under attack

Chris Owalla
KENYA

Human rights defender Chris Owalla was attacked by armed individuals in February when attending the funeral of journalist Dickens Ochieng Wasongain. He suffered severe injuries to his knee, elbow, chest and back, and was robbed of his clothes, money and personal belongings. Owalla has been targeted previously for his work as a vocal advocate for social and environmental justice and a staunch campaigner against corruption and mismanagement of public funds. It's believed the latest attack related to his work into government mismanagement of funds.

Lutfiye Zudieva
UKRAINE

In February, human rights defender and journalist Lutfiye Zudieva had her house raided by law enforcement officers in Crimea after she was accused of "abuse of freedom of mass information" due to Facebook posts she made in 2021. During the raid, officers refused to answer questions or allow Zudieva support from lawyers or relatives. Zudieva, a prominent activist who has supported political prisoners in Russian-occupied Crimea through her role at the Crimean Solidarity organisation, was taken in for questioning after the raid and now faces a court hearing.

Rocío San Miguel
VENEZUELA

Rocío San Miguel, a human rights defender and lawyer from Venezuela, was detained in February under charges including treason and terrorism. Five of her relatives were also detained. San Miguel specialises in military issues and is the president of the Citizen Watchdog on Security, Defense and the Armed Forces which monitors Venezuela's commitment to human rights. She has previously been targeted by the state for her work, suffering constant harassment from the Venezuelan government as well being defamed on numerous occasions.

Yasser Eljuboori
IRAQ

Irish citizen Yasser Eljuboori was illegally detained by Iraqi authorities at the end of February while travelling back to his home in Ireland and was prevented from contacting his family. Eljuboori is a renowned anti-corruption activist and it is believed that the charges relate to this work, as well as his criticism of the Iraqi prime minister on social media. His wife has revealed that he was seriously mistreated during his days in detention; he was beaten, and blindfolded and his mistreatment led to him staging a hunger strike. Fortunately he returned home safely on 6 March.

Ink spot

THIS CARTOON, BY Nasrin Sheykhi, highlights the plight of Iranian rapper Toomaj Salehi.

Salehi was released from prison on bail last November following a year in prison, including 252 days in solitary confinement, on charges over the content of his music and for his support of the protests against the death of Mahsa (Jina) Amini.

Salehi, who was awarded the 2023 Arts Freedom of Expression Award by Index, then used his social media channels to share details of his torture while inside. He was violently rearrested two weeks later and is now back in prison with his future uncertain.

Nasrin Sheykhi is an Iranian cartoonist who moved to the USA because of the political situation in her home country.

She has been drawing cartoons since she was 15 and has won around 40 international awards and published a book called Paper Faces.

World In Focus: Yemen

As the country grapples with an all-encompassing civil war, free speech is one of the many casualties

1 Sanaa
Since the outbreak of the Yemeni war in 2015 following years of unrest and uprisings, freedom of speech and expression in the country has seen a rapid decline. The Houthis, a Shia Islamist military group, seized control of the Northern Yemeni government in 2015 following a popular uprising and dissolved the parliament, setting up a Supreme Political Council in Sanaa to fill the political vacuum. However, deposed President Abdrabbuh Mansur Hadi maintains that he is still in power. Democracy itself has been sacrificed to make way for the conflict as politics is put on hold; elections are long overdue, and many state institutions have ceased functioning altogether. The state remains trapped in a bitterly violent and seemingly endless conflict, with no political freedom for its citizens.

2 Aden
To be a journalist in Yemen is to put your life on the line. Media freedom in the country has spiralled during the current conflict, with a number of reporters facing extortion, imprisonment or even death for their work. According to the Committee to Protect Journalists, at least 35 journalists and media workers have been killed. Several high-profile incidents occurred in the port city of Aden in the south of the country; reporters Saber al-Haidari and Rasha al-Harazi were killed by car bombs in 2023 and 2021 respectively, while in June 2020 freelance journalist Nabil al-Quaety was shot and killed by unidentified gunmen. These are just a handful of incidents demonstrating the danger involved in reporting on the atrocities currently taking place in Yemen.

3 Hadramout
The Hadramout region encompassing much of eastern Yemen has a terrible record when it comes to free speech. Journalists have been detained, threatened and forced into hiding as a result of the crackdown on independent media by local authorities. One of the most recent examples of this is the ordeal of Hala Badawi, a freelance journalist who was detained in December 2021. The Hadramout authorities claimed she had been involved in terrorism after she shared a post on Facebook accusing the director of the education ministry bureau in the province of corruption. Other reporters have been made to sign statements promising not to cover political protests in the region, showing the extent to which governing bodies are attempting to silence those who pose a threat to their power.

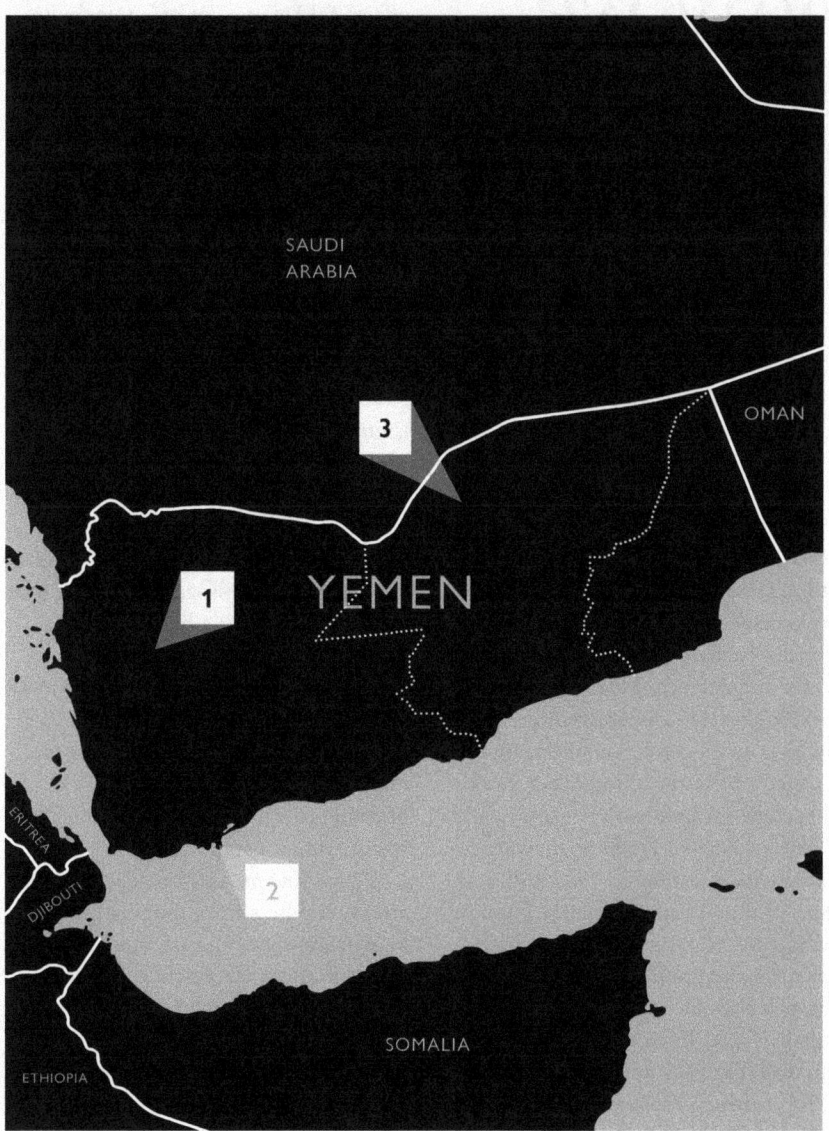

The Index

TECH WATCH

Why we need to ban spyware

MARK FRARY looks at the continuing fallout from the Predator Files revelations

IN LATE FEBRUARY, Politico reported that Predator spyware had been found on two devices used by members of the European Parliament's subcommittee on security and defence. Meanwhile, the Greek publication Documento recently showed how the device of an employee of Greece's Ministry of Internal Affairs had become infected with the spyware.

The existence of Predator spyware became widely known in 2023 with the release of the so-called Predator Files. Its extensive use to target rights defenders, journalists and politicians is gradually being revealed. However, Cybersecurity company Cisco Talos says Predator has been available since at least 2019.

The year-long Predator Files project was based on thousands of confidential documents obtained and analysed by Germany's Der Spiegel, France's Mediapart and analysed by Amnesty International's Security Lab, under the European Investigative Collaborations umbrella. The project revealed that Predator spyware was developed by Intellexa Group, a network of companies based in various jurisdictions, both inside and outside the EU, and founded in 2018 by former Israeli army officer Tal Dilian. The group includes Ireland's Thalestris, North Macedonia's Cytrox, WiSpear from Cyprus, which specialises in wi-fi interception, and Israel's Senpai Technologies.

When the Predator Files were released, Amnesty revealed that those targeted by the spyware included the president of the European Parliament, Roberta Metsola, the president of Taiwan, Tsai Ing-Wen, US Congressman Michael McCaul, US Senator John Hoeven, the German ambassador to the United States, Emily Haber and French MEP Pierre Karleskind.

In the recent case reported by Documento, a woman at Greece's Ministry of Internal Affairs had received a series of text messages suggesting that a video taken from a hidden camera had been given to the independent investigative blog Edolio 5 and invited her to click on a link to read an accompanying article. Other similar messages followed. All had the goal of trying to make her click on the link which would install Predator.

This is known as a one-click attack. It differs from the other well-known spyware Pegasus which, more disturbingly, is a zero-click attack – your device can be infected without actively doing anything. This can be achieved by taking advantage of flaws in messaging apps such as WhatsApp. Amnesty's Security Lab says that a loophole in the way that Apple's iMessage delivers image previews has been exploited in this way. As such exploits are discovered, the spyware companies move on to new areas. In September 2023, Haaretz reported that they were now exploiting the system that delivers personalised adverts to users.

With both types, once a device has been infected, a malicious actor can access everything on the device.

In July, the US government added Intellexa and Cytrox to its "Entity List for Malicious Cyber Activities", which makes it subject to export restrictions. Announcing the news, the State Department said: "The misuse of these tools globally has also facilitated repression and enabled human rights abuses, including to intimidate political opponents and curb dissent, limit freedom of expression, and monitor and target activists and journalists."

In October, the collaboration's findings were independently confirmed by Canada's Citizen Lab. They highlighted a tweet by Albanian politician Etilda Gjonaj, which quote-tweeted another tweet by US ambassador to Albania Yuri Kim. A user commented on the post with a link to an article entitled "UK aims to deter Albanian refugees with 'make clear the perils ad' campaign". The headline was chosen to encourage people to click on the link which came from a website called the South China Post, effectively designed to look like the South China Morning Post. Those clicking on the link would start the installation of Predator. ✖

Mark Frary is associate editor at Index

Hay Festival
Hay-on-Wye

23 May — 2 June 2024

Book Now
hayfestival.org/hay-on-wye

Talks · Books · Ideas · Debates · Music · Workshops

Join us for 11 days of different

GALLERIES AROUND THE WORLD ARE AT AN ETHICAL CROSSROADS.

Can they resist pernicious corporate and political influence?

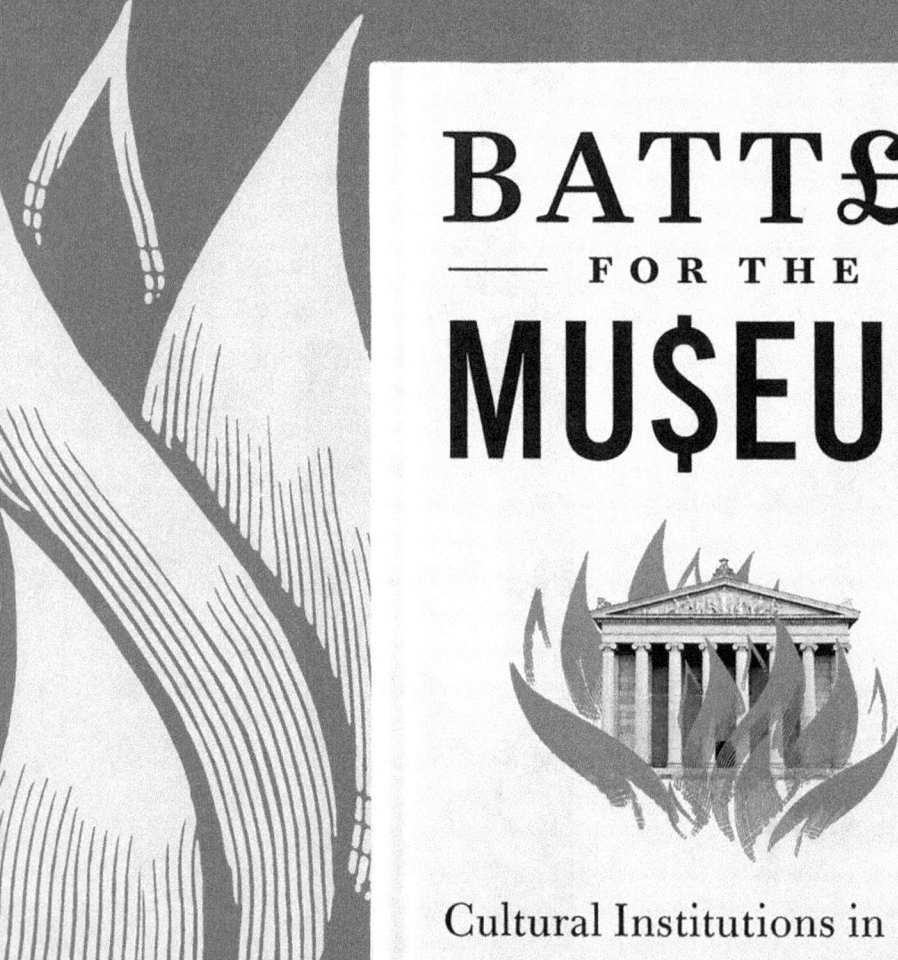

OUT IN MAY 2024

hurstpublishers.com

FEATURES

"Considering the battle somewhat won in the USA
(although pro-choice groups continue to fight),
several anti-rights groups are attempting to influence
and support other countries in doing the same"

THE ANTI-ABORTION ROADSHOW | REBECCA L ROOT | P.28

Just passing through

Crime runs rampant in Guatemala and people are too afraid to speak up. **EDUARDO HALFON** reports from a recent trip on the modern-day, gun-toting highwaymen holding up drivers amongst others

1. The egg

In Guatemala, you'll be driving around the capital city when suddenly a raw egg will come crashing down on your front windshield. Your initial reaction, of course, after letting loose a few choice words of insult, will be to turn on the wipers, which will only make matters worse. The raw yolk will smear all over the glass and you won't be able to see anything through the yellowish stain. A block or two later, you'll be required to pull over and get out of the car to somehow try to clean it off. And the comrades of the egg-throwing car thieves will be waiting for you, pistols in hand.

2. The petrol station

You'll be driving along a Guatemalan highway, possibly in some lush and deserted mountainous region, when you'll realise that you're running low on fuel. You'll stop to fill up at the first petrol station you encounter, something that in the country is done by an attendant. It's always a full service, never self-service. The attendant will usually be kind and well-mannered. He'll check your tyres and your oil; he'll clean your front and rear windshields with a dirty rag. And so, after paying for the petrol and also giving him an appropriate if not generous tip, you'll promptly be back on your way. A few kilometres later, however, you'll notice that you now have a flat tyre, and you'll be forced to stop to change it on the side of a completely barren part of the highway.

Just then, almost miraculously, a motorcycle with two men will appear in your rearview mirror. In no time at all, they'll reach the spot where you're stranded and get off their motorcycle and ask if you need help changing the tyre. And you'll be relieved and thankful, before seeing them pull out a couple of handguns and steal everything you have.

What you never noticed, naturally, was that the motorcycle had been parked behind the petrol station, lying in wait, while the well-mannered attendant placed a large, sturdy nail in front of one of your tyres as he squatted down and pretended to check it for air.

3. Pablo

It's commonplace to be robbed as you're sitting in your car at a red stoplight in Guatemala City. Someone will stick a knife through the open window, or maybe tap on the window with a gun, and hurriedly demand that you hand over your phone, your watch, your rings and necklace, your wallet or purse. My aunt never noticed the fist that flew in through the semi-open window to swipe away her designer sunglasses, and which also left her with a black eye.

Some Guatemalans, to fend off these hasty robberies, have grown accustomed to either making a half-stop or just simply speeding through a red light, especially in seedy neighbourhoods late in the evening. Others have adopted a more lawful and also more creative approach: they've taken to driving around the city with a full-body mannequin sitting in the passenger's seat. They actually go out to a store and buy a mannequin and dress him up. It's always a man. Then they sit him in the passenger's seat with his seatbelt well fastened. Why? The robbers, the reasoning goes, will think twice if they see that you're not driving alone, that there are two people sitting in your car at the stoplight, even if one of those people is just a big plastic doll.

Once, a bright and attractive middle-aged woman told me that, to make the ruse more convincing, she would drive around the city speaking to her mannequin, whom she called Pablo.

4. The cleaner

One warm April morning in 2022, three plain-clothes police officers turned up in the lobby of my parents' building in Guatemala City looking for a man who worked there named Jeremías. They wouldn't say much to the rest of the maintenance personnel and security staff, just that they needed to talk to him and ask him a few questions. But the officers were repeatedly told by the building's employees that he was nowhere to be found, although they all knew exactly where he was hiding.

Jeremías had been working in my parents' building for more than 10 years. He seemed to always be there, sweeping a hallway, using a squeegee to wipe clean the elevator mirror, minding the reception desk at the lobby, or so it appeared to me each time I travelled

> Someone will stick a knife through the open window, or maybe tap on the window with a gun, and hurriedly demand that you hand over your phone, your watch, your rings and necklace, your wallet or purse

PICTURED: Getting robbed while you are stuck in traffic is commonplace in Guatemala City

back to the country from Nebraska or Paris or Berlin or wherever I was currently living, and came by to visit. He was shy and softspoken. He was considerate without being sentimental; attentive without being nosy. Never troublesome, my father said of him, by which he meant that Jeremías was submissive and obedient. He'd always greet me kindly, "*Buenos días, señor Halfon*", and then ask with a reluctant smile if I was living back in Guatemala or if I again was just passing through, and I'd inevitably answer that just passing through. Now I understand, however, albeit in hindsight, that his simple and almost perfunctory question was all too ominous.

That warm April morning, Jeremías had been sitting at the reception desk of the lobby when he saw the police officers on the screen of the security camera video, standing and smoking outside in the street in front of the building. He somehow knew, or perhaps guessed, that they were there looking for him and so he immediately bolted for the basement and hid in a small utility closet, crouched down among all the mops and brooms and several dingy buckets.

The police officers were frustrated by the employees' curt and evasive answers. As always, Guatemalans have been silenced by decades of oppression and mistrust and the paralysing fear of speaking out. The police now insisted on talking to some of the tenants, including my mother and father. They went from apartment to apartment, knocking on doors and asking questions. But none of the tenants could help in locating Jeremías. None knew where he was or even if he'd showed up to work that day. Ultimately, after a couple of tense hours of threats and prying around, the officers gave up and left the building and the tenants closed the doors of their apartments, and all the employees went back to work.

Jeremías stayed hidden in the utility closet the rest of day. He waited until it was dark outside and could be sure that the police officers were no longer in the neighbourhood. He then stood up and walked out of the closet and strolled out of the building and there, in the middle of the street, he was quickly tackled and captured by the police officers, who'd been waiting for him in unmarked cars.

Everyone's first thought was that Jeremías had been wrongly apprehended, something all too frequent in the country. Usually because of a personal vendetta, or because of a bureaucratic mistake, or more likely because a corrupt government official cooked up false charges against someone in order to then ask for a hefty bribe. It would take weeks to find out what had really happened.

After repeated phone calls and letters and several expensive lawyer visits, the building's tenants were finally informed that Jeremías was being held at the state penitentiary of Mazatenango, a city on the coastal plain leading to the Pacific Ocean, for his involvement in a series of what locals have termed, in Spanish, *secuestros exprés*. Or express kidnappings.

This is how they work:

> You get a call from a kidnapper who will tell you that someone is presently following the car of one of your family members, your elderly father or your teenage daughter or maybe even your wife

You get a call from a kidnapper who will tell you that someone is presently following the car of one of your family members, your elderly father or your teenage daughter or maybe even your wife, and they will proceed to shoot your father or daughter or wife unless you deposit a given sum in their bank account within an hour, usually the equivalent of no more than a couple of thousand dollars. As proof, the kidnapper will first mention all your family member's personal information, complete name, home address, business address, phone number, driving licence number; the kidnapper will then tell you exactly what clothes your family member is wearing at that very moment and on which road of the city your family member is currently driving; lastly, the kidnapper will give you a precise description of the make of your family member's car, including the model, the year, the specific colour, the plate number and any unique features like visible dents or scratches or bumper stickers. All so it's made clear to you that your father or daughter or wife has, in a sense, already been kidnapped and is being held captive in their own car and without them knowing it and perhaps even with a shotgun pointed at their head from a few cars away, and will only be released from that cruel and strange form of captivity if you swiftly and discreetly make the required deposit.

For years, Jeremías, our softspoken Jeremías, had been the money man in these operations. It was his personal bank account that the gang of kidnappers had repeatedly used for receiving all the ransom payments.

So, *señor* Halfon, he would say with a shy smile, here to stay or just passing through?

Just passing through, Jeremías. Always just passing through. ✖

Eduardo Halfon is an award-winning writer originally from Guatemala, whose books have been published in over 15 languages

FEATURES

Exporting the American playbook

Book banning is gaining ground in Canada but an army of authors and campaigners are ready to fight back, writes **AMY FALLON**

ABOVE: Authors Ronnie Riley and Robin Stevenson (below) have had their work restricted

WHEN CANADIAN NON-BINARY and queer author Ronnie Riley discovered they'd been "shadow banned" last November they were horrified. But it was a matter of sooner rather than later.

"I felt absolutely horrible, but I knew it was a possibility," said the Toronto-based writer, who spent several years trying to get their debut novel aimed at middle graders, Jude Saves the World, published. In the book, 12-year-old protagonist Jude Winters is non-binary and has ADHD.

"I've experienced my share of transphobia and queerphobia, but this was particularly heartbreaking," Riley told Index.

"Connecting with kids is one of the reasons most 'kidlit' authors write, and being denied those opportunities because of queerness is outrageous. It's queerphobic. Homophobic. Transphobic."

"Shadow banning" is a broad definition usually attributed to social media posts, describing the limiting of a particular user's content without their knowledge.

Riley's discovery came via a leaked memo on Reddit that they then saw on social media. According to the circular, the Waterloo Catholic District School Board, about 95km outside Toronto, had decided to place books that were part of the Forest of Reading (FoR) programme but "don't align with the Family Life curriculum" in the professional (Pro) section, where they are not immediately available to students.

The board added that "before JK [junior kindergarten] grade 6 students may borrow these books from the library, a teacher must provide the Catholic context because students haven't been instructed in the Family Life curriculum yet". Jude Saves the World was one of four works targeted from the FoR programme.

When Index contacted WCDSB this January, the organisation's senior manager of communications, Lema Salaymeh, told Index that all FoR titles have since been reclassified as fiction or picture book, adding: "This reclassification is part of our larger initiative to review the books catalogued in the Pro section. This effort will be conducted in tandem with our ongoing, scheduled review of our Library Collection Development Administrative Procedure, ensuring our collection remains dynamic and inclusive. By making these changes, we hope to create a more welcoming and diverse environment for all our students, including those who identify as 2SLGBTQIA+."

This re-classification of books came after a co-ordinated pushback by the FoR, Scholastic Canada, The Writers' Union of Canada and others.

Unlike in the USA, where book challenges are regular and well-documented, not as much data on book challenges and bans is available in the more liberal Canada. But as part of an "aggressive" response to censorship, a library challenges database is now in its early stages of creation, thanks to the Centre for Free Expression at Toronto Metropolitan University, and so far it contains more than 600 entries, according to centre director James L Turk. The records start in 2010 and include books that have attracted complaints for perceived violence, illegal behaviour, sexism, racism against indigenous people, age inappropriateness and anti-Christian content. While most targeted items have stayed on the shelves, many have been relocated.

In Canada, the growing problem "should be seen as the canary in the mine metaphor – that book banning and book challenging is a starting place for worse things to come," Jen Ferguson, a Michif/Métis and white author and activist warned an audience at Vancouver Writers Fest in October.

"In the US, I have no rights over my reproductive system, which is fucking bananas," said Ferguson, who now lives in Iowa. The challenges in the USA are part of a "wave of fascism" involving fights that "mostly we've won" in →

CREDIT: Juliana Johnson (Riley); Stephanie Hull, Centric Photography (Stevenson)

Canada. But the writer added: "For the non-readers this is a sign of things to come. I think that's why we need to care, all of us, and why we need to organise."

Richard Beaudry, co-ordinator of the University of British Columbia's Teacher-Librarianship programme, who has equipped librarians to deal with book challenges for the past two decades, said that there was no doubt that bannings had increased in Canada.

In February 2023 in Calgary, Alberta, a preacher stormed a drag queen storytime event in a library, with bystanders saying he shouted "religious jargon" and transphobic slurs. He was arrested and charged with hate-motivated crimes. Three months later, in Manitoba, the Brandon School Division rejected a call to remove books on sexuality and gender identity, including titles such as It's Perfectly Normal, an illustrated book by Robie H Harris for 10-year-olds and above which explores puberty and sex.

In September, some schools in Peel, Ontario, even removed all books published before 2008 – including the Harry Potter and Hunger Games series – as part of an "equity-based book weeding process" undertaken by the Peel District School Board, aimed at making sure library books were inclusive. It was immediately halted by Ontario education minister Stephen Lecce, who didn't respond to Index's requests for comment.

Peel District School Board told Index that it follows "library weeding guidelines set by the Canadian School Libraries Association" which direct it to keep books "relevant to the student population, inclusive, not harmful, and support the current curriculum from the Ministry of Education".

It said the guidelines also "[direct] teacher-librarians to consider weeding books that may be misleading, 'ugly' [in poor condition], superseded, trivial, irrelevant, and elsewhere easily available".

While most challenges are never successful, they still cause harm.

"You're killing a little piece of the literary ecosystem, doing it out of view," said Brendan de Caires, executive director of PEN Canada. He highlighted that those demanding the bans were targeting relatively new authors such as Riley, who are "low-hanging fruit" in their eyes.

With elections lined up in Canada for 2025, book bans are likely to increase. After nearly a decade in power, Liberal Prime Minister Justin Trudeau is tipped to lose to Conservative leader Pierre Poilievre. The populist, who backed the 2020 Freedom Convoy protesting vaccine mandates, is favoured by groups behind the bans such as Liberty Coalition Canada, Save Canada and Parents for Parents' Rights, according to Turk. None of these groups responded to requests for comment.

"The threats to intellectual freedom are coming from all sides, and everyone bringing them is well intentioned in their own mind, even if their behaviour is reprehensible in the rest of our minds," Turk said.

In Canada, most of these organisations instigating book challenges are relatively small and inspired by Judeo-Christian principles. Miramichi Freedom Warriors, which last year distributed thousands of photocopies of a library's "requests for reconsideration" forms to fundamentalist Christian churches, created more challenges for the New Brunswick Public Library Service in four months than in the entire history of public libraries in the province, Turk said.

The largest and best-funded

OPPOSITE: Protesters clash with counter-protesters outside a drag queen storytime event hosted by the Ottawa Public Library, Canada

network behind the potential bans is Action4Canada, which has "taken the game plan of Moms for Liberty", said Beaudry. Inspired by the sophisticated political operatives who receive huge sums of money from right-wing US foundations, the self-described "grassroots movement" was launched in British Columbia by Tanya Gaw and Valerie Price. They now claim to have nearly 100 chapters across the country.

Vehemently opposed to the Sexual Orientation and Gender Identity programme (SOGI 123) introduced in British Columbia in 2016, Action4Canada's tactics include a "notice of personal liability", which they encourage individuals to send to their local libraries. It claims that books are violating the Canadian Criminal Code on child pornography, warning that people could be charged and jailed. The network's "urgent actions" include petitions to ban SOGI 123 and a library appearance by drag queen Freida Whales in Kelowna, a city in the province. Action4Canada did not respond to repeated requests for comment.

Queer Canadian author Robin Stevenson described them as "very much following that American playbook – 'Let's get Conservatives elected to school boards. Let's challenge books. Here are the lists of books you should object to'".

One recent talk Stevenson scheduled was open to a whole Canadian school board but just one class attended. "The teacher told me her colleagues were too nervous about parents complaining so they didn't include their classes," she said, adding that there is a reluctance to put queer books on the shelves: "Librarians are telling me that they're buying my book but they'll keep it in the counsellor's office."

Stevenson added that there was also a "hesitancy to invite queer authors to schools in the first place",

> Librarians are telling me that they're buying my book but they'll keep it in the counsellor's office

as they wanted to avoid backlash. This ultimately costs LGBTQ+ authors, who make a large part of their living from these talks, Jen Ferguson told the VWF.

In the supposedly tolerant east side of Vancouver, librarians are today flipping through young adult novels to look for hateful and harmful comments, Jen Ferguson warned the audience at the VWF, recounting a conversation with a librarian. The Vancouver Public Library, however, said it had no evidence of this.

Perhaps one of the biggest prices will be the "unwritten books", added de Caires. "You can't even see consequences [of bans] until you have a decade of books not being written because the people who would have written them have been scared off."

At the VWF, Ferguson stressed that "those of us who are furious about book banning and book challenging, we're just slightly less organised" than those demanding the bans. For fellow panellist Winnipeg-born trans author Casey Plett, there's a silver lining: "This is something that you can solve."

For the CFE, it has meant arming people with information about each challenge – what's being targeted, why and how – via its database, plus creating profiles of previously challenged books to be ready for "wild claims". The CFE has been encouraging all libraries to add to the list. "[Librarians] have never historically treated a tweet or an email as a challenge," said Turk, adding that getting them to understand this had been tricky. While he said public libraries in Canada had mostly been "the absolute strongest defenders of intellectual freedom", the pressures in schools was different. Other than in British Columbia, most don't have teacher-librarians, often leading to "terrible positions" adopted by school boards.

Turk added: "We have to do a lot of public education about this, talking about why [just] because you don't like something or you find it offensive, that's not grounds to say that nobody else can see it."

But the resistance movement is gaining ground, with Beaudry saying that Canada is picking up the pace against censorship. He points to specialised work against book challenges from the intellectual freedom committee at the Canadian Federation of Library Associations, and said that in the last elections, almost everybody who ran as a trustee against the SOGI programme and LGBTQ+ books in schools was not elected. And of all the authors Index spoke to, every single one said they would remain defiant and refuse to be silenced. ✖

Amy Fallon is an Australian-Canadian journalist

The couple and the king

Eswatini's king rules the country with an old-school iron fist. **CLEMENCE MANYUKWE** speaks to the widow of Thulani Maseko about his battle for fair representation

FEATURES

LEFT: Swazi lawyer and government critic Thulani Maseko appears in court in 2014

THE VOICE OF Tanele Maseko, the widow of assassinated Eswatini human rights lawyer Thulani Maseko, conveys the conviction of one determined for justice. She wants to ensure that attempts by her husband's killers to create a wall of silence around her and her country are not successful.

Maseko's killing in the presence of Tanele and their children while at home on 21 January last year has come to symbolise his country's struggle to free itself from the jaws of a repressive, absolute monarch.

Speaking to Index days after the first anniversary of her husband's assassination, Tanele, a human rights activist herself, said: "They would like to silence me because of what Thulani believed in, his ideals, what he stood for. What he was eventually killed for, I will continue to fight for. So as I seek justice for my husband, I continue also to call for democratic reforms in the country."

Maseko's cold-blooded killing by unknown gunmen came seven years after he delivered a speech – Using the Law to Defeat a King – at the Oslo Freedom Forum. That king, Mswati III, was crowned in 1986, aged 18. He took over from his father, who had ruled the country since it gained independence from Britain in 1968.

In his Oslo Freedom Forum speech, Maseko criticised the king for using "supremacy and absolutism to suppress the people". He also spoke about how he was twice incarcerated – in 2009 for sedition for saying that a bridge next to the palace should be named after two activists who died on the bridge, and in 2014 for contempt of court for criticising the judiciary. Maseko spoke about how he was taken to court in leg irons, like an animal, and how his wife, young son, family and friends who visited him were abused.

He said that being out of jail did not mean he was free. Still, he was not going to give up on values he held dear, even if there was a price to pay for the truth.

In the years between his Oslo speech and his assassination, Maseko continued to use the law to challenge Africa's last repressive, absolute monarchy.

After King Mswati unilaterally changed the country's name from Swaziland to Eswatini, Maseko approached the High Court in 2018, arguing that there was no public consultation and the move undermined the constitution. No verdict had been issued at the time of his death.

Maseko also challenged the Suppression of Terrorism Act and the Sedition and Subversive Activities Act. The courts said the laws violated freedom of expression and association. Although he won, the government appealed. The matter is still pending.

His death, a symptom of efforts to turn criticism of the monarch into a taboo, left a huge gap in the fight against tyranny in Eswatini.

Under Mswati, demands for sweeping reforms have been met by state violence. In 2021, for example, there was a bloody crackdown on pro-democracy protests that reached a peak on 20 June, when about 500 people took to the streets in the city of Manzini. During the unrest, dozens were killed in an act that highlighted just how systemic the silencing of dissent has become.

Following Maseko's assassination, the monarch accused Tanele of "removing evidence at the crime scene". A government spokesperson also warned that her "remarks" tracing Maseko's assassination to the monarch's doorstep were treasonous.

Tanele told Index that her husband was killed hours after King Mswati delivered a speech saying he had mercenaries to deal with dissenters. →

They would like to silence me because of what Thulani believed in, his ideals, what he stood for

INDEXONCENSORSHIP.ORG **21**

She added that there had been no progress in investigating the assassination, and there had been attempts to silence her.

"If the government is not guilty they should investigate, get the killer and prove us wrong and not insinuate that what I'm saying is treasonous. If they are not involved why not investigate? Why is it that this investigation is taking so long?" she said.

"That was not merely a killing. It was an organised [killing] and that was a professional [job]. So it's quite upsetting for a government spokesperson to say my statements were treasonous. If they have anything to prove, they need to work on this case. The investigation has to be transparent, it has to be open so that they cleanse their name."

She told Index that since her husband's death, surveillance on her has continued. According to Tanele, they have even used artificial intelligence and a drone.

Tanele wants the UN to intervene to ensure an independent investigation, and she said it must appoint a special rapporteur for southern Africa to deal with human rights violations in her country and others, such as Zimbabwe and Lesotho.

Human rights lawyer Sibusiso Nhlabatsi, who regarded Maseko as his mentor, told Index that freedom of expression in Eswatini remained a mirage. He said the constitution guaranteed and protected the right to freedom of expression, including the rights of the press, but in reality several laws limit these rights. These include the Suppression of Terrorism Act, the Sedition and Subversive Activities Act and the 1973 King's Proclamation.

"Swaziland is silently a military state. Human rights [are at their] lowest ebb. What the constitution guarantees in the bill of rights is not practically true," he said.

Speaking of the many people who have called for democratic change either being in jail (where they're denied bail) or being in exile, Nhlabatsi said: "The state has been selective in its approach to the unrest. While those who are calling for democratic change have been arrested, the security personnel involved in mass killings have not been arrested."

Nhlabatsi said people are calling for democratic changes that will allow the participation of political parties in elections.

"The people want the prime minister elected by the people with the monarchy playing a minimal (ceremonial) role and staying off politics. There are also extreme views that call for the abolishing of the monarchy," he said.

He added that although he had not seen any direct threats to his life, he did not feel safe due to his closeness to the late Maseko and his human rights work.

In a statement to mark a year since Maseko's assassination, Vongai Chikwanda, Amnesty International's deputy regional director for east and southern Africa, said the silence surrounding the case was deeply troubling, reflecting a broader pattern of impunity and disregard for human rights in Eswatini. The statement said rights defenders should be allowed to carry out crucial work without fear of reprisals.

"The authorities must also ensure the wellbeing and safety of Thulani's widow and other members of his family," said Chikwanda.

Tanele is waiting for the day such words become action. Until then, she and those who were close to Maseko will live in fear. ✖

Clemence Manyukwe is a freelance journalist based in South Africa

> While those who are calling for democratic change have been arrested, the security personnel involved in mass killings have not been arrested

Justice on hold for the man who fought for justice

THULANI MASEKO, BORN in 1970, was known as a loving husband and father. He was a committed member of Eswatini's Methodist church, a devoted human rights defender and an ally to LGBTQ+ people and other minorities. For the latter Thulani was persecuted throughout his life. He was first arrested in 2009 and again in 2014. Both times upon his release he immediately returned to his work defending human rights and calling out state corruption, even filing a legal challenge against the King himself for undermining the Constitution after he changed the country's name from Swaziland to Eswatini. In 2016, for example, he said: "We shall never surrender, for we know there is a price to pay for the truth."

On 21 January 2023, Thulani was shot dead in the living room of his own home in front of his wife and family, mere hours after King Mswati threatened pro-democracy activists in a public speech. There was uproar in the international community; the UN condemned the killing, with the High Commissioner for Human Rights Volker Türk declaring that the world had lost a "true champion and advocate for peace".

Despite calls from numerous human rights organisations to investigate Thulani's murder, nobody has yet been held accountable for the killing. Tanele continues to fight for justice on behalf of her husband.

FEATURES

Obrador's parting gift

Mexico's president refuses to risk letting the press tarnish his legacy – and he has created the perfect propaganda machine, writes **CHRIS HAVLER-BARRETT**

ENTERING HIS SIXTH and final year in power, there is little to say about Andrés Manuel López Obrador's term as Mexican president that has not already been said. The charismatic politician has dominated the country's politics for almost three decades.

Fuelled by his two failed earlier runs for the top job – for which he blames the media – Amlo, as he is ubiquitously known, has spent his entire presidency as an advocate for the poor, uplifting Mexico's most impoverished regions, renationalising key industries and building infrastructure fit for the modern era.

Or so he claims.

There is some truth in these statements, but the tidal wave of success that he portrays is the result of a complex and aggressive propaganda machine that comes disguised as openness and accountability. What is supposedly the cornerstone of a free press in Mexico has instead been transformed into a tool to defend Amlo's ego and legacy.

It is impossible to discuss his six years of leadership without discussing the *mañanera*. Every weekday morning begins with the same ritual, almost without exception.

Obrador invites journalists to a press conference, where he and his cabal of trusted advisers from the military and cabinet lecture them for hours. These conferences are broadcast via the internet and appear on television, on the radio and in newspapers. The best photos, where Amlo flashes a mercurial smile or looks down benevolently from the podium, are shared on his personal webpage.

After decades of highly restricted access, the chance to sit and directly question the president was initially perceived to be an irresistible opportunity that few could pass up, winning him plaudits from the international community.

Former UK Labour Party leader Jeremy Corbyn appeared as a guest of honour, calling the briefings "very impressive and [showing] a degree of openness in government that is not found in many countries of the world".

As praise for the new order began to fade, however, the *mañaneras* took on a different tone.

Joel Aguirre, a veteran Mexican political journalist, has been following successive presidencies for two decades.

"I think that the relationship of the press to President Amlo during these last five years of government has been very tense, it has been difficult – perhaps more than we've seen in previous governments," he told Index.

This is a serious issue in a country where dozens of journalists have been killed by cartels in the same period – something the government has shown little desire to investigate.

Despite this initially positive outlook, the president now heckles and attacks journalists who oppose him, denouncing them and their work.

Aguirre said: "At the start of this government [Obrador] said: 'They might speak badly of me, but we must let them speak'."

But Aguirre adds that the press conferences are now reduced to little more than "the gallery of the president [and] a platform for propaganda".

Aguirre is direct in his assessment of what has happened.

"The *mañanera* has lost all its value," he said. "In years gone by we would have loved this, because there was no way to confront the president. Now you can, but only if you belong to a selected outlet.

"The *mañanera* began to be attended by journalists who are affiliated with the president. They ask 'fashionable' questions, things that are very obvious. The entry list is controlled to prevent a journalist from being too critical or saying the wrong things so the president is unable to evade his question."

The *mañaneras* now serve only to allow Amlo to pontificate on his successes. Defiance of the new order is met with public humiliation, exclusion and defunding.

Few incidents illustrate what it has become better than the recent press conference in which Amlo publicly shared the phone number and contact address of New York Times journalist Natalie Kitroeff, who had written an article suggesting that he had been investigated by the US Drug Enforcement Agency for ties to the Sinaloa cartel.

"The moment he published her details, he exposed her to fanatics – to agents of the government. That was an attack on [press] freedom," Aguirre said.

Amlo simply claims that his "moral and political authority are above the privacy act" and denied any risk to journalists in Mexico, claiming such risks are the fabrication of "special interest groups".

Jan-Albert Hootsen, the Mexico representative for the Committee to Protect Journalists, has been reporting on press freedom from the country since 2016. He told Index this:

"Unfortunately, it's getting increasingly hard for us to convey

The president now heckles and attacks journalists who oppose him

→ the urgency of the situation if the narrative is controlled by the president." He added: "A very substantial fanatical following basically considers journalists to be legitimate targets of online threats and online harassment and continues to maintain this idea that if the press is attacked it's their own fault."

Additionally, collusion by media outlets is financially rewarded.

Traditionally, the government has funded the press by paying media companies to run public awareness campaigns and carry announcements. But the arrival of Amlo has shaken this up, with only favoured (uncritical) outlets now receiving funding, which involves reporting on the *mañaneras* without questioning the provenance of the information provided.

Likewise, without access to the *mañaneras* – which begin early in the morning and often shape the day's national news – unfavoured sources are completely frozen out of access to the country's top politicians.

Without access to real accountability, and by creating a system of "transparency" that serves only to broadcast propaganda, support for

ABOVE: President Obrador raises the hand of a journalist during one of his trademark mañaneras

Amlo has become almost cult-like. Official government surveys show an extremely high level of trust and approval in the president, whose primary support base is highest amongst the very young, the elderly and those with no education.

Trust in the media has collapsed, with a Reuters report suggesting that the number of Mexicans who believed the news declined from 50% during Amlo's first year in office to just 36% last year.

"The numbers of the support amongst the Mexican public are exaggerated. The federal government attempts to push the narrative that there's about 70% of Mexicans [who] support him," Hootsen said.

"That's an incredibly high number in the sense that it's just not believable. It's not realistic. That said, he still has a very, very untraditional loyalty amongst his followers," he added, explaining that many of Obrador's followers are deeply distrustful of the traditional media and largely use social media.

"It is fairly easy for him to bypass the sort of traditional rules and relationships that you could have with the press, which allows him to develop these very toxic, very – I would say at this point – dangerous narrative that we saw [with the Kitroeff incident]," he said.

Ultimately, Obrador's party, Morena, is trying to create an environment where there is no need to use the media at all.

"There is a certain very 21st-century component about it, which is the use of social media trying to bypass the regular communication channels such as the media in order to control the narrative," Hootsen said.

The proliferation of cheap internet access in Mexico during the Amlo presidency has also made it easier for those in rural areas to access news via social media, rather than legacy media outlets.

As well as attacking freedom of expression, Amlo uses his briefings to circumvent electoral regulations.

"At this point [it's] very clear that the mañanera and all the activities that the president's organising around them are a form of campaigning for him. So, he's in constant violation of electoral law," Hootsen explained. "What he's doing now is attacking the national electoral institute, trying to lower its budget, trying to handicap it up to the election."

And despite leaving the top job later this year, Amlo will remain involved in the running of the country.

While he has publicly stated that he intends to retire to his ranch in his home state of Tabasco, his Morena party is a broad political church united only by respect for his vision and leadership.

His successor as head of the party, Claudia Sheinbaum – almost certain to win the upcoming presidential election – is somewhat quieter, more calculated and a shrewder political operator.

But Hootsen is unsure that this change of leadership will bring any changes from the system currently in place. "She's not going to be able to make sufficient substantial changes in six years to make Mexico a noticeably safer country for journalists and human rights defenders," he said. "I think that's an illusion."

While Sheinbaum does not go for the bombast and confrontation so beloved by her political mentor, the avoidant, deflective anti-media environment employed by Morena means that things are unlikely to get any better for the press, who remain stuck between deadly threats from organised crime and a government that intends to totally defund them unless they agree to publish propaganda. ✖

Chris Havler-Barrett is a freelance journalist who was based in Mexico until recently

> The moment he published her details, he exposed her to fanatics, to agents of the government

Silencing the faithful

Violence against practitioners of Afro-Brazilian religions is on the rise in Brazil. **SIMONE DIAS MARQUES** interviews some of the few who aren't too scared to talk

THE INSTANCES OF discrimination, violence and intolerance towards followers of Afro-Brazilian spiritual traditions are escalating. In 2023 alone, reported cases were up by 80% on the previous year, according to the Ministry of Human Rights and Citizenship. Among the most frequent victims of these violations were adherents of Umbanda, Candomblé and other African-derived spiritual traditions. Now people increasingly live in fear, speaking in hushed tones about what is happening to them and even more quietly about the fact they are of a certain faith.

Many cases of violence against those from traditional communities associated with the Black diaspora involve vandalism of their places of worship. A recent example was the attack on the Mãe Oxum monument in Porto Alegre on 25 January.

The monument, considered a historical and cultural site in the southern city, was vandalised with graffiti saying "pagan" and "Christ lives". The perpetrators have not yet been identified by the police.

In 2022, a survey conducted by the Ilê Omolu Oxum centre and the National Network of Afro-Brazilian Religions and Health (Renafro) consulted 255 Pais and Mães de Santo (priests and priestesses) across Brazil.

The findings revealed that 60% of terreiros (Afro-Brazilian religious centres) in the country had been vandalised at least once in the preceding two years, while 80% of the interviewed leaders reported that members of their communities had suffered some form of violence motivated by religious racism.

"It is unacceptable that in 2024 we have to face such barbarity. We are outraged," the president of the Federation of Afro-Brazilian Religions (Afrobras), José Antônio Salvador de Iemanjá, told Index.

"It's hard to put into words, as it strikes at the heart of faith, which is the most sacred thing in this world. If we let this crime go unpunished, there may be further actions of this nature, culminating in increasingly violent acts."

It is not uncommon for people to be insulted and attacked, and terreiros to be closed due to neighbourhood hostility, but in some cases this has escalated to murder, as was the case with Mãe Bernadete, a yalorixá (priestess) who was fatally shot in Bahia last year.

"Physical assaults also occur in the streets, such as when Uber drivers refuse to transport people dressed in religious attire or carrying sacred instruments. I have personally experienced situations where drivers refused to take me because of this," said Janine "Nina Fola" Cunha, a member of GeAfro (the Centre for African, Afro-Brazilian and Indigenous Studies at The Federal University of Rio Grande do Sul) and an anti-racist activist for more than 30 years.

The rights to practise Afro-Brazilian religions are both recognised and guaranteed by Brazilian legislation. As stated in the federal constitution, "Freedom of conscience and belief is inviolable, ensuring the free exercise of religious worship and protecting places of worship and their liturgies".

Last year, a law was brought in equating the crime of religious insult with racism, once again protecting religious freedom. Anyone who obstructs, impedes or employs violence against any religious person or practice now faces up to five years in prison.

But data shows a large gap between constitutionally granted rights and the treatment of minorities.

"Several laws address not only religious freedom but also freedom of worship, especially those aimed at traditional African-derived peoples. Despite that, these laws are not duly respected," said lawyer Pai Tiago de Bará-Onilù, legal co-ordinator of the Independent Association in Defence of Afro-Brazilian Religions. He explained that widespread fear had come to characterise those who are part of these faiths, and that they feel too vulnerable to openly express their beliefs.

According to Cunha, the increase in aggression is mainly due to the rise of the extreme right, with many factions allied with neo-Pentecostalism. "This combination has resulted in a noticeable increase in violence against our religiosity, often with impunity, as some sectors view defending their religion as legitimate at the expense of others."

Bàbá Hendrix de Òrúnmìlà, a historian, afrotheologian and babalorixá (priest), attests to the rise in violence in recent years. "The best definition is not intolerance; it's religious racism. Many religions face religious intolerance, but none experience the racism that we do. The neo-Pentecostal sector actively persecutes us, especially after [former president Jair] Bolsonaro's last government regime; the persecutions have become more intense, with a kind of permissiveness to openly declare hatred," he told Index.

He uses an example to explain: the time when an evangelical pastor kicked

 The belief that 'the demon is always external' has led to tragic consequences

ABOVE: Candomblé women celebrate Black Awareness Day at the monument to Zumbi dos Palmares in Rio de Janeiro

an image of Our Lady of Aparecida (the patron saint of Brazil).

"There, it was Christian against Christian, a matter of intolerance. But what happens to us goes beyond religiosity; it's not just about religious practice – it's racism. We have our freedom of religion curtailed; it is prohibitive to express ourselves without being exposed to acts of religious racism," Òrúnmìlà said.

"In recent years, there has been a period of convergence of political and religious conservatism, which attributes salvation through politics. This led politicians to legitimise racism and violent acts propagated by religious conservatives.

"This will generate, for example, the 'Traffickers of Jesus' in Rio de Janeiro – criminals converted to Christianity who expel the Mães de Santo from the Rio Hills with machine guns at their heads, accusing them of being 'of the devil'."

The motivation that links the devil to African traditions is convenient, as it externalises evil and justifies its eradication. The belief that "the demon is always external" has led to tragic consequences, including the murder of Mother Mukumbi in 2013 and others across different regions of the country, as well as the desecration, vilifications and fires at terreiros, said Òrúnmìlà.

In Brazil, associating religions of African origin with devil worship has a long history, reaching back to the end of the 19th century when Catholicism became Brazil's dominant religion. Then with the rise of the neo-Pentecostal churches – and through the press – African religions were demonised further. It all happened in tandem with more general racism. The view was that everything with black roots was inferior while white was superior.

"It is, indeed, persecution. First, the terreiros were persecuted by a segment of the Catholic Church. Then, between the 1970s and 1980s, the Pentecostal churches began to emerge who intensified the persecution, to the point of this becoming religious racism," said Renafro co-ordinator Bàbá Diba de Iyemonja.

"But there was also the weight of institutional racism on the part of the state through the security apparatus, such as the police."

Religious racism has intensified with social media. By 2014, Index On Censorship had already documented numerous incidents, including the dissemination of 16 videos on YouTube that encouraged violence against practitioners of Candomblé and Umbanda. These videos, posted by the Igreja Universal do Reino de Deus, a neo-Pentecostal church, remained online until a protracted legal dispute finally forced their removal. Some experts and leaders of terreiros have labelled the phenomenon as religious terrorism.

According to the 2010 census by the Brazilian Institute of Geography and Statistics, about 600,000 people in Brazil identify as followers of African-derived religions.

It's thought these numbers are under-reported, which shows how high the stakes are now to be open about practising a religion that isn't mainstream. ✖

Simone Dias Marques is a Brazilian journalist, translator and writer

PICTURED: People protest against abortion in Spain, a country which some say is exporting anti-rights ideology

FEATURES

CREDIT: Marcos del Mazo / Alamy

The anti-abortion roadshow

Conservative groups in the USA are taking the campaign against reproductive rights global, using money and influence to silence, writes **REBECCA L ROOT**

NOT CONTENT WITH implementing abortion bans on their home turf, groups from the USA are increasingly exporting their ideologies and their funding to other countries.

"There's always been a proliferation of anti-rights, anti-gender groups, especially under a Republican administration ... but in the past five years, it has been mind-blowing because it seems like it's getting more intense, more scaled up and more sophisticated," said Fadekemi Akinfaderin, lead of global advocacy for change at Fòs Feminista, an international alliance for sexual and reproductive health and rights.

"They definitely have gotten a →

> Politicians now won't push for increased abortion access because they are being threatened by the faith groups

INDEXONCENSORSHIP.ORG **29**

→ bit more wind beneath their sail since Dobbs."

US anti-rights groups claimed a victory when the landmark 1973 Supreme Court ruling of Roe v Wade, which ruled the right to abortion was protected under the constitution, was repealed with the Dobbs v Jackson decision in 2022. This now affords individual US states the right to regulate abortion as they see fit.

As a result, 14 states have criminalised abortion no matter the circumstances, six have "severely restricted" it and several others have imposed restrictions to some degree. In the 18 months since abortion access was repealed, women have faced criminal charges for trying to get abortions and had their health jeopardised, forced to continue with unsafe pregnancies.

Considering the battle somewhat won in the USA (although pro-choice groups continue to fight), several anti-rights groups are attempting to influence and support other countries in doing the same, experts told Index. Some of those groups include Family Watch International (FWI), Alliance Defending Freedom International (ADF) and Human Life International. Index has repeatedly approached Human Life International for comment and has not received a reply.

Both mifepristone and misoprostol, used for the medical management of abortions, are listed on the World Health Organisation's essential medicine list. Member states are obligated to provide access to these drugs.

Without access to safe services, women may seek out other options which endanger them. Each year 39,000 women across the world die following unsafe abortions.

According to Katy Mayall, director of strategic initiatives at the Centre for Reproductive Rights, the trend over the last 30 years has been an increasing liberalisation of abortion laws. Only four countries – the USA, El Salvador, Poland and Nicaragua – have re-criminalised abortion compared with more than 60 that have made it easier to access.

But research conducted by a coalition of health advocacy groups has revealed that more than 50% of participants believed the situation in the USA has empowered anti-abortion movements in their countries, while a 2024 report by Fòs Feminista found that there had been an increase in anti-rights groups' use of disinformation campaigns since the Dobbs decision.

As a result in India, for example, there have been anti-rights protests across the country for the first time, alongside calls for the government to overturn the legislation allowing for medical abortions.

"[There have been] judicial appeals to ban abortion and restrict access within the Indian courts system by faith-based opposition groups," one report participant is cited as saying. "This has never been an issue for India but is emerging [or] growing into one post- [the repealing of] Roe."

In Africa, the East African Community Sexual and Reproductive Health Bill 2021, which would increase access to sexual and reproductive services in six countries, stalled following the Dobbs decision. Angela Akol, director of Ipas Africa Alliance, told Index that legislators who work to increase access to safe abortions and contraception began holding meetings with US anti-rights groups. Conversations around pushing the bill forward have since resumed, but the bill is yet to pass.

Since the US decision, the narrative, Akol explained, is that abortion is a Western concept and if the USA is no longer pursuing it, why should Africa?

In Nigeria, where abortion is permitted only when the mother's life is at risk, abortion guidelines had been created to support healthcare providers. Following the Dobbs decision, a local opposition group – which Akinfaderin said had ties to pro-family, Christian NGO FWI – spread disinformation (which FWI denies), claiming that Nigeria was going to legalise abortion. Pressured by an upcoming election, politicians recalled the guidelines, which are yet to be re-disseminated.

And in Malawi, Emma Kaliya, a local pro-choice activist and director of the Malawi Human Rights Resource Centre, said such groups have "invaded" the country from the USA, at times holding conferences on the issue without including local activists.

"We are tired of this influence that comes from elsewhere. They want to manage a small country like Malawi," she said. "It's becoming an issue of religious fundamentalism, where now they are taking charge of everything and pushing back on everything – especially on the rights of women."

She said politicians now won't push for increased abortion access because they're being threatened by faith groups, who will withdraw their support.

Aware of the threats, Akol said there had been talks on how to better protect what's known as the Maputo Protocol, which promotes and protects reproductive rights for the 44 out of 55 member states across Africa which have ratified it.

"We've realised that if Maputo failed, a lot of us would be naked," she said. But pushback against the

> Such organisations are strategic – often setting up offices in key European locations with strong links to human rights

anti-rights agenda has to come from countries themselves, she warned, adding that any foreign interference would only feed into the idea of abortion as a Western narrative and form of colonialism.

FWI denied opening new offices in Africa and told Index: "There is an individual spreading misinformation to various media outlets regarding the work of FWI in Africa. We do have a Family Watch team that has been working for several years on the continent." They also said they "strongly promote the protection of life in the womb and at all stages, but that is not our main focus in Africa".

Such influence isn't being exerted only in Africa. A report produced by the European Parliamentary Forum for Sexual and Reproductive Rights (EPF) explored how religious extremists generate funding to restrict human rights, and found that $81.3 million of "anti-gender" (sometimes known as "pro-family") funding was sent from 10 US Christian-right NGOs or think tanks to European organisations between 2009 and 2018. That figure continues to grow and $120 million was estimated to flow into Europe in 2022 – a $40 million increase since 2018.

The same names and organisations keep coming up globally, Neil Datta, executive director of the EPF, said on the sidelines of the Women Deliver conference in Rwanda last year.

Such organisations, Datta said, are strategic – often setting up offices in key European locations with strong links to human rights such as Brussels, Geneva and Strasbourg. "They are intent on influencing," he said.

ADF International and the European Centre for Law and Justice (ECLJ), in particular, are recorded in the EPF's report as having played a role in more than 30 legal cases since 2013 that were said to undermine human rights in Europe. Datta explained that the groups were working with local lawyers to hunt down historical legal cases

> Such groups have "invaded" the country from the USA, at times holding conferences on the issue without including local activists

that can then be used in court to tackle legislation that currently allows for abortion access.

This strategy was legitimised by the rollback of Roe v Wade in the USA and now it's being implemented globally, he explained – adding that these groups not only focus on abortion access but also the rights of the LGBTQ+ community.

Index has approached ECLJ for comment multiple times but the group has not responded.

ADF told Index: "Given the strong ideological bias of the European Parliamentary Forum for Sexual and Reproductive Rights against our organisation, the credibility of any of their allegations should be called into doubt … It is wholly inappropriate for them to be cited as a source commenting critically on our funding, when their reporting is both inaccurate and hypocritical."

They added: "ADF International is committed to safeguarding everyone's fundamental rights, including the right to life for every mother and baby. We are also committed to protecting the right of everyone to freely express their beliefs. That right only really means something if it protects the right to speak even when others disagree."

Last year, Uganda criminalised identifying as homosexual which, according to Datta, was a direct result of such interference. Similar attempts to influence the law have been made in Kenya, Malawi and Tanzania, he added.

Both LGBTQ+ and reproductive rights are recognised as fundamental by the Universal Declaration of Human Rights. Yet pro-choice groups working to strengthen rights are being silenced by donor-imposed restrictions.

Akinfaderin explained that many large organisations don't allow their donations to go towards lobbying, and with much of women's health playing out in the hands of legislators that's not helpful. In contrast, anti-rights groups rely more on individual donors, which tend to have less restrictive funding that allows them to lobby all they want.

"Take the shackles off funding. Remove these certifications [and] lobbying clauses, so that the resourcing is truly transformative and can help us to get to the goal that we want," Akinfaderin said. "We know that we cannot sit on the sidelines in terms of issues related to policy and law-making. We know we can't sit on the sidelines when it comes to elections."

Elections are set to take place in 64 countries in 2024, and if more conservative governments come to power this could have a bearing on abortion access.

"Spain is one to continue to watch because we do know that there are a lot of anti-rights organisations from Spain that are now setting up offices and registering branches in Africa," she said, citing conservative advocacy group Citizen Go as an example.

To ensure such groups' impact is at a minimum, she called for more feminist groups and organisations to engage with electoral processes. "We can't just sit and hope for the best [and] hope we get progressive governments." ✖

Rebecca L Root is a freelance journalist based in Bangkok

PICTURED: Covid conspiracy theorists march in London

The woman taking on the trolls

The journalist **MARIANNA SPRING** spends her days investigating trolls and meeting their victims. She speaks to **DAISY RUDDOCK** about what it's like on the frontlines of this murky world

MARIANNA SPRING IS no stranger to the perils of calling out those in power. As the BBC's disinformation and social media correspondent, she spends most of her time in a world of conspiracy theories and trolls, which has the unfortunate consequence of making her some high-profile enemies.

"Elon Musk trolled me, which was not very fun!" she told Index laughing. "He says the media don't hold the powerful to account. Well, Elon Musk is one of the most powerful people in the world and I really wanted to hold him to account, but when I tried to, he triggered loads of online abuse! I don't know where that sits on the freedom of expression scale."

Spring is speaking to me ahead of the launch of her new book, Among the Trolls: My Journey Through Conspiracyland, which was released this March, and which delves into the unforgiving world of misinformation and conspiracies. She has had to put up with significant pushback because of the nature of her investigations. Some 80% of all escalated online abuse received by the BBC is directed at her alone. Despite this, Spring says she won't hold back.

"I try really hard to not let that happen, because I think the goal of online abuse is to discourage you from doing your job," she said. "It's effectively a tool that's used to try and silence you."

However, that doesn't mean the abuse hasn't made an impact.

"I love investigating this world because I think it's really important and it's exciting and interesting, but it makes you a real lightning rod for hate and criticism," she admitted. "Criticism is totally fine, but not hate and trolling."

One thing she has considered, she said, was quitting X. "X has changed phenomenally for me in terms of how my feed works. A lot of the people who send me abuse now have blue ticks, so what they send me is very visible," she said. "Pile-ons are more frequent than they were before."

Spring's book could hardly have come at a more appropriate time, which she admits is a "slightly happy accident". The recent rise of AI has exacerbated the problem of misinformation, and with four billion people heading to the polls in a historic electoral year the issue has become even more urgent.

"The timing of this feels like we're coming to the end of one chapter and entering a new one, but with all the problems of the old chapter," she said.

Spring worries that as difficult as disinformation is to identify and control now, AI will only worsen the problem. She points to one example she investigated recently of an AI-generated recording of London mayor Sadiq Khan circulated online. "Audio is so much harder to verify, you can't spot the seven fingers that the AI-generated videos or photos have. I think that's my biggest worry going into this election year."

Addressing the problem of misinformation in the age of social media seems like an almost insurmountable task. Spring's approach is to zone in on the most harmful and viral cases and reach out to the individuals involved to interrogate their feelings. "I hope that by taking one case at a time I can help people understand how that's chipping away at what we actually take for granted in our society", she said.

Naturally for someone calling out misinformation, Spring is heavily involved in conversations about free speech. "A lot of the stuff I investigate is inhibiting and affecting other people's freedom of expression. If you are being repeatedly hounded or abused online, your freedom of expression is compromised," she said. "I focus on a lot of the most extreme disinformation where it's incredibly clear cut that it's false. What I'm doing is exposing the harm that these extremist truths can cause rather than policing what people say or don't say."

Not everyone sees it that way. The online trolls who relentlessly follow her claim that by fact-checking mistruths she infringes on people's right to free expression, an argument with which Spring firmly disagrees.

"I find it quite hard to understand when people imply that I'm somehow inhibiting freedom of expression, yet they think it's fine to send death threats and hate to a reporter in a democracy. I think if you believed in freedom of expression you wouldn't be doing that!" She added: "I'm always happy for people to challenge what I have to say."

In her book, as in her work at the

> What I'm doing is exposing the harm that these extremist truths can cause rather than policing what people say or don't say

BBC, Spring addresses misinformation in various forms. As well as speaking to individuals harmed by fringe groups such as disaster trolls claiming that the 2017 Manchester Arena bombings were staged, she looks at wider issues including state-sponsored disinformation campaigns. She identifies Russia as being "particularly active" in this regard.

"There's some really good analogies about Russia and disinformation, this idea of it being this firehose of mistruths. It's just a constant bombardment of stuff that's often quite brazen, outright lies," she said.

Her investigations of Russia resulted in her being included in a list of UK individuals who have been sanctioned by the state, which she says hinders her work. "[Russia] said that me and other journalists that I've worked with have been put on this list for being like George Orwell's 1984, and I was thinking this all feels so topsy-turvy!"

With such a growing profile, the BBC correspondent is aware of the risk of amplifying the very misinformation she seeks to confront. When weighing up whether to highlight an issue, Spring tells me she considers two factors: how viral has it gone and is it causing real world harm? "We should always be asking ourselves both of those questions, because I think there's a risk that people jump on it and then you become part of the problem."

Spring is particularly mindful of this because she worries that a fringe view can suck in anyone. "We all think we are immune to misinformation and actually I just don't think any of us are." ✖

Daisy Ruddock is editorial assistant at Index

LEFT: Marianna Spring's new book, which builds on her work at the BBC concerning misinformation and conspiracy theories

Broken news

MEHRAN FIRDOUS follows **FAHAD SHAH** in the weeks after his release from prison, revealing how India's targeting of Kashmiri journalists has taken a personal toll

FAHAD SHAH, THE founder and editor of the now banned independent news outlet The Kashmir Walla, was detained in February 2022 after publishing a report about an encounter in Pulwama. He was released and rearrested repeatedly before being charged under the Unlawful Activities Prevention Act, an anti-terror law. Shah was released on bail from Kot Bhalwal Jail in Jammu on 23 November. He is now free but his publication is not.

"It has honestly been very difficult to come back and a struggle to reintegrate into normal life. Spending 21 months in prison mentally affects you. It has not been an easy journey. Since I have returned, my focus has been to recover from trauma and try to get used to normal life. It has been a tough task every day," Shah told Index.

He has struggled to find a good support system. He spends time with family and friends who take it in turns to keep him company in between running their own lives. He knows that he can't expect people to keep listening to his problems forever, and that eventually he will have to restart his life.

Shah described the myriad hardships he faced while in prison. He said: "First, being away from family and friends takes a toll on your mental health. [You] suddenly leave behind your normal life and find yourself trapped in a hole. You always want to come out of it but you don't find anything that can bring you out."

Despite this, he has learnt several things from his time in prison. "I became more patient with life," he said. "I learned to let it go or to deal with major crises with patience. It also made me realise what matters actually in life and why desires make us keep running after materialistic aspects of life. We don't really live life but we create a sense of life around us. And when something falls apart, we feel hollow. Prison taught me to survive on limited resources and find hope even in the darkest hours."

For years, journalists in Indian-administered Kashmir have faced numerous threats, often caught in the crossfire of conflicting parties. When India revoked the region's semi-autonomy in 2019, their situation became much worse.

A year later, the government - which has been accused of numerous human rights abuses in Kashmir - announced a media policy that allowed it to examine every piece of news and censor content. Since then, several journalists have been targeted by strict anti-terror laws that include questioning and arrests.

Shah's publication of 12 years issued a statement in August 2023 saying →

> My heart sank when I heard about the ban on The Kashmir Walla. I was left to cope with the news on my own because there was no one in the prison to console me

PICTURED AND OVERLEAF: Fahad Shah, editor of The Kashmir Walla, returning to his life in Jammu and Kashmir after many months in prison. His paper has been shuttered following a sweeping attack on indepedent media and critical figures ordered by the Indian government

FEATURES

I still feel sad when I think back on the times I spent there with my co-workers, since The Kashmir Walla was like a second home

→ that it had become inaccessible in India due to an order from the Ministry of Electronics and Information Technology to block its website under the Information Technology Act, without any prior notification.

"My heart sank when I heard about the ban on The Kashmir Walla. I was left to cope with the news on my own because there was no one in the prison to console me," Shah said. "There's no doubt that processing this development will take time. I still feel sad when I think back on the times I spent there with my co-workers, since The Kashmir Walla was like a second home to me. It provided many young journalists with an invaluable platform to develop, learn and make a living."

When it comes to the restoration of The Kashmir Walla, Shah hasn't given it much thought. He has been out of prison for only a few weeks, and the task of bringing back a banned publication is taking a backseat for now.

"My current priority is my personal recovery. I aspire to return to my office and work with my team again, but at the moment waiting is my only option, for now it feels like a dream to work at The Kashmir Walla office again." ✖

Mehran Firdous is a freelance journalist based in Kashmir

Who can we trust?

Ecuador is facing a crisis of trust, and drugs are at its root. **KIMBERLEY BROWN** reports

IN ONLY A few years Ecuador has gone from being one of the safest countries in Latin America to being one of the most dangerous, as criminal gangs controlling the international drug trade unleash violence. At the same time, corruption scandals have rocketed, with dozens of government officials, lawyers, judges and journalists being linked to criminal gangs. The effect on freedom of expression is profound.

Two months after taking office last November, President Daniel Noboa responded to this violence by declaring a war on 22 armed groups he calls "terrorists".

He immediately deployed the military onto the streets and into prisons, and claims he is taking back the country. But experts are sceptical that brute force can fix Ecuador's systemic problems or rectify the damage that's already been done to some of its key institutions.

Both journalists and the judiciary have faced increasing threats and pressure to co-operate with criminal gangs over the years, with no safeguards from the state. In extreme instances, these take the form of murder.

Two main events brought Ecuador's violence into focus on the international scene: the public assassination of journalist and political candidate Fernando Villavicencio as he was leaving his campaign rally in August last year, and the takeover of the TC television news station by masked armed men in January, while the station was broadcasting live. Both these events were flagrant attacks on freedom of speech and the media, instilling fear into Ecuador's population.

Press under stress

These threats aren't new. In 2023, local press freedom group Fundamedios registered 265 attacks against journalists and freedom of speech, including incidents such as letter bombs and assassination attempts, making it one of the most violent years on record for media workers.

Another press freedom watchdog, Periodistas Sin Cadenas (Journalists Without Chains), said death threats directed at journalists increased by 275% in 2023 from the previous year. Last year, nine journalists were forced to abandon their homes and secretly relocate abroad or to other parts of the country – something Ecuadorian journalists have never had to face before.

Karol Noroña was one of the first forced to flee the country last March. She had long been covering the deadly riots taking place inside Ecuador's prisons and the dynamics of armed groups behind bars for national media. But after two sources connected to criminal gangs told her that her name was on an assassination list, she fled the country.

"I had access to chats and audios where I heard that this person was going to kill me. They had identified where I lived, where I worked, had photographs of me," Noroña told Index.

Dagmar Flores, of Fundamedios, says most threats and attacks are directed at journalists covering organised crime or corruption among local officials. As a result, many have abandoned these topics altogether, choosing to focus on lifestyle and entertainment rather than local news.

LEFT: The armed men who shocked Ecuador by storming the TC Television station in a violent raid were detained and presented to the press

→ This has left major gaps in information, particularly about communities along the coast where violence by criminal groups has been the strongest, and in some inland provinces that lie along the drug routes or where illegal mining is prominent, she says.

One journalist, who asked not to be named, told Index about a hyper-local news website they started years ago from their town on the coast, where they published community complaints and eventually began reporting on murders and questioning the municipal authorities.

They were forced to leave their home after receiving severe threats and dodging an assassination attempt. Today, they continue to work in journalism occasionally from their new location, but they've stopped reporting from the streets, rarely publish with their real name, and refuse to mention violent murders in order to avoid future threats.

The first murder of journalists in the country happened in 2018, when two of them and their driver were kidnapped and killed, shocking the country.

Families and colleagues continue to pressure the state for answers, saying an adequate investigation was never conducted. Susana Morán, a journalist and representative with Periodistas Sin Cadenas, says the impunity from this case set a dangerous precedent for journalists, who are living with those repercussions now.

After years of pressure from press organisations, the government finally created a security mechanism last year to protect journalists facing threats, called the Mechanism for the Prevention and Protection of Journalistic Work. Though still in its initial stages, Flores says it lacks the major funding needed to be implemented properly. One of the mechanism's biggest challenges will be gaining the trust of journalists, as most don't report threats they receive or seek help from the state, concerned that local authorities are often connected to organised crime.

> Most threats and attacks are directed at journalists covering organised crime or corruption

An unjust system

While journalists feel gagged, a lack of trust in authorities and government institutions is another key issue in the country, where corruption scandals break on a regular basis. The most recent came to light in December, when the Attorney General's Office arrested nearly 30 government officials, lawyers and judges for their connections to organised crime in an ongoing investigation dubbed "Metastasis". The investigations don't bode well for Ecuador's justice system, which is already facing increasing scrutiny by the public. One Ipsos poll from 2023 showed less than 12% of the population trusted the justice system.

But deep-seated corruption is only one of the crises facing Ecuador's judicial system. In recent years, lawyers, judges and other judicial operators have themselves faced increasing threats and attempts on their lives for the work they do. In 2023, the Observatory of Rights and Justice of Ecuador (ODJ) counted four assassinations, as well as 28 attacks against lawyers, judges and judicial operators – everything from attempted killings, bomb threats and direct threats and intimidations. The year before, six judicial operators were killed, according to the ODJ.

The most recent victim was prosecutor César Suárez, who was known for taking on corruption cases. He was killed in the coastal city of Guayaquil in January, just days after he began investigating the takeover of the TC television station.

Judge Heidy Borja, president of the Ecuadorian Association of Magistrates and Judges in the province of Guayas, received a death threat in 2022 from a criminal gang who demanded she work for them and rule in the gang's favour in applicable cases.

If she refused, they told her, they would put an explosive in her car, and then named several family members. She reported the threat and worked from home until the state finally gave her protection. She has been accompanied by bodyguards ever since.

Sadly, not everyone receives this protection, and that's one of the main problems, said Borja. If the state can't guarantee the safety of judicial workers, that makes them more susceptible to falling prey to these kinds of threats, and ultimately corruption, she added.

Little wonder, then, that Ecuador sees a high rate of impunity in all sorts of crimes, ranging from car theft to assassinations, depending on whose interests are involved, explained José Andrés Murgueytio, a lawyer and special projects co-ordinator with the ODJ.

Last August, Margaret Satterthwaite, the UN special rapporteur on the independence of judges and lawyers, said in a press release that she was "dismayed by the great vulnerability of justice officials" in Ecuador, adding that officials needed to do more to protect judicial workers. But the reaction from the presidential office has been the opposite, choosing to denounce judges publicly or label prosecutors defending accused gang members as "terrorists".

This public shaming often puts the lives of judges and prosecutors more at risk, said Murgueytio. Meanwhile, none of the recent presidents have denounced the many crimes and threats terrifying the judiciary or the media.

In Ecuador, no one knows who to trust anymore. ✖

Kimberley Brown is a freelance journalist based in Ecuador

53(01):38/40|DOI:10.1177/03064220241243217

The cost of being green

Environmental campaigners in Vietnam are being locked up on spurious charges, writes **THIỆN VIỆT**

WHEN HER FORMER boss, a prominent environmentalist, was arrested on the trumped-up charge of tax evasion, Phương was saddened – but not surprised.

"[Anyone who enters] the non-profit sector in Vietnam would envision that it is a risky profession," she said, asking to use a pseudonym for fear of government reprisals for speaking to foreign media.

Phương, a sustainability advocate, said Vietnam's non-profit sector had been on high alert since 2021, when the arrests of other prominent environmental advocates on exactly the same charge began in earnest.

"It was a self-fulfilling prophecy," she said, adding that the silencing tactics used against leaders are little known outside the sector, including cyber-harassment and delayed approval processes for projects.

"We know that our leaders endured a lot of harassment [they] did not share with us because they wanted us to focus on our work," she said. After the NGO's closure in 2022, Phương had to find another job.

Other notable targets have included Mai Phăn Lợi, head of the Centre for Media in Educating Community, Đặng Đình Bách, director of the nonprofit Law and Policy of Sustainable Development (LPSD), and Ngụy Thị Khanh, director of the Green Innovation and Development Centre and Vietnam's first recipient of the prestigious Goldman Environmental Prize.

In June 2022, Khanh was sentenced to two years in prison on the charge of tax evasion, related to her 2018 prize. Human rights groups condemned the sentence and her early release in May 2023 – just a few months before the meeting between US president Joe Biden and Vietnamese president Võ Văn Thưởng to upgrade the countries' relations to a comprehensive strategic partnership – was not mentioned in domestic media.

The US Department of State called for Khanh's release in 2022, but during Biden's visit the US president was accused of sidelining human rights issues, causing serious concern for Vietnamese activists.

In September 2023, Hoàng Thị Minh Hồng, director of Change, a non-profit organisation advocating for sustainable development which was closed in late 2022, was imprisoned for three years for tax evasion.

In the same month, Ngô Thi Tố Nhiên, executive director of the Vietnam Initiative for Energy Transition (Vietse) was arrested without charge. After spending five days in detention, police charged Nhiên with "stealing, buying, selling or destroying the seal or documents of a state agency or organisation". She remains behind bars, without trial.

After her arrest, Vietse was forced to shut down, as was Bách's organisation.

Within the space of two years, Vietnam had arrested six prominent environmental activists on trumped-up tax evasion charges. The arrests show increasing censorship of environmental advocacy, and concerns have been raised by the international community, including the EU.

The arrests are on the extreme end of the scale of oppression but are representative of a broad trend of how environmental rights defenders across the Mekong region are treated.

Those seen to be linked with foreign actors – often the case for environmental NGOs sponsored by international organisations – are at a higher risk of being targeted.

The activists arrested under tax charges were all part of the advisory group for ensuring human rights in the EU-Vietnam free trade agreement. They were all working closely with international donors to push for the shift away from coal, Vietnam's primary energy source, towards clean energy.

A state-affiliated journalist who wished to remain anonymous told Index about the media coverage of the activists, saying: "It is not possible to report positive things on Vietnamese NGOs if they disagree with the government."

In a country that has committed to net zero emissions by 2050, and where environmental protection was once perceived as non-political, something has shifted. In recent years, campaigning on environmental issues has increasingly been seen as a direct challenge to the Communist Party of Vietnam (CPV).

In 2010, bauxite mining in the Central Highlands gained significant national attention when national hero and former military commander General Võ Nguyên Giáp wrote an open letter to then prime minister Nguyễn Tấn Dũng, expressing his opposition to the government's plans and citing concerns about environmental damage, potential →

> **Within the space of two years, Vietnam had arrested six prominent environmental activists on trumped-up tax evasion charges**

harm to ethnic minorities and a perceived threat to national security.

The letter prompted widespread discussion and debate across the country about bauxite mining and Chinese investment. Eventually, by exerting pressure on the Vietnamese government, the anti-bauxite activists successfully influenced a policy change that prohibited Chinese investors from exploiting those reserves.

This wasn't the only furore around bauxite mining. In 2009, Cù Huy Hà Vũ, who holds a doctorate in law and is son of the former minister of culture Cù Huy Cận, initiated legal action against Dũng for granting exclusive rights to a Chinese mining company at a bauxite project in the Central Highlands – a move which he said violated national defence law, cultural heritage law and environmental law.

"The court dismissed the lawsuit, [ruling] that in Vietnam the prime minister could not be sued," said Vũ, who is now in exile in the USA.

In response, Vũ invoked the Administrative Procedure Law, which allows legal action against every subject of administrative decisions, including the prime minister. The court remained silent.

In 2010, Vũ filed a second lawsuit against Dũng, claiming that his signing of a new decision which prohibited class-action petitions against local and national governments was a violation of the constitution.

In a third move against the authorities, Vũ defended 2,000 Cồn Dầu parishioners in November 2010, taking on one of the most powerful commissars in the country who wanted to expropriate an entire parish for an eco-tourism project.

A month later, he was arrested without charge. Then, after a hasty trial, he was sentenced for conducting and circulating anti-state propaganda.

Social media, however, has also created a space for change, pushing activism forwards. The CPV has a tight grip on traditional media, but in recent

ABOVE: Mines have become an unlikely battleground in Vietnam's crackdown on free expression, as climate activists campaigning for clean energy are locked up on spurious charges

years digital platforms have allowed citizens to join together in a rallying cry to expose environmental issues.

In 2015, students, artists, intellectuals and residents joined forces to successfully oppose Hanoi's decision to cut down 6,700 trees in the capital — an unprecedented move in a country where any act of criticism might be classified as "regime opposition".

The following year, approximately 70 tonnes of dead fish were found along more than 200km of Vietnam's central coastline. When Formosa, a Taiwanese company, denied any responsibility for the incident, protests took hold of the country, even though such acts were deemed illegal. Authorities dispersed demonstrators and many were briefly detained.

> The court dismissed the lawsuit, ruling that in Vietnam the prime minister could not be sued

Then, in 2019, the climate strike finally came to Vietnam. Residents of Ho Chi Minh City poured onto the streets to participate in the worldwide action, calling for immediate and significant action to combat the pressing climate challenges faced by their city – particularly the dual threats of rising sea levels and air pollution. As the protest built, domestic media remained silent.

The CPV was not tolerant of those peaceful protests. Many protesters were dispersed, harassed and attacked by the police. The draft laws on associations and demonstrations, despite both domestic and international pressure, have not been passed by the National Assembly.

Dr Peter Bille Larsen, a senior lecturer and researcher at the University of Geneva, studies the intersection between environment and social justice.

"I've always been impressed by the collective and personal drive, commitment and willingness to protect the environment and the country," he said. "Indeed, where international ideas may fail or be poorly adapted, homegrown solutions are urgently needed.

"From local officials to national heroes like General Võ Nguyên Giáp, readiness to stand up for the environment is a precious national tradition that needs protection."

Despite smear campaigns and prison sentences against Vietnam's most influential environmental defenders, people are still speaking up. An international campaign has been launched by the Vietnam Climate Defenders Coalition to demand the activists' urgent release, and to put an end to the threats facing environmental campaigners.

Guneet Kaur, an activist from river protection organisation International Rivers who co-ordinates the coalition, believes that wrongfully incarcerated environmental defenders such as Bách and Hồng paved the way for Vietnam's Just Energy Transition Partnership, which is a funding agreement supported by international partners to help emerging economies. Keeping them behind bars is putting that future at risk.

"Their unjust and arbitrary incarceration cannot lead to any form of just energy transition. [But] it has led to a chilling effect on the environmental movement and civic space in Vietnam," Kaur said. ✖

Thiện Việt is a journalist from Vietnam

Who is the real enemy?

South Korea's president is pushing the nation to the right and invoking fears about North Korea to silence his critics.
RAPHAEL RASHID reports

WRITING A POEM about a unified Korea, a place where everyone has a home, a job and access to free education and healthcare, might seem harmless. But for 68-year-old South Korean Lee Yoon-seop, such a dream landed him in prison for 14 months under South Korea's National Security Act.

His case reignited the fiery debate: does the act stifle freedom of expression and promote censorship?

In 2016, Lee submitted his poem about a North Korean-style socialist, unified Korea to a North Korean state-run competition. Access to such sites is both not allowed and blocked in South Korea, accessible only from abroad or through a VPN connection. His entry, The Path to Unification (which you cannot access easily in South Korea as the link is blocked), was chosen as one of the winning works in the competition.

During the November 2023 sentencing of Lee, who had already served prison time for a similar offence, the court said that he had "produced and distributed a significant number of subversive expressions that represent North Korea's position, glorify and praise it, and threaten the existence and security of the country or the basic liberal democratic order over a long period of time during the period of repeated offences, so it is inevitable that he will be severely punished".

Human rights organisations slammed the ruling, calling for all charges against Lee to be dropped.

"Although there is a unique geopolitical situation in [South Korea], it does not justify unlawful restrictions on freedom of expression that violate international standards," said Amnesty International's East Asia researcher Boram Jang. "Writing a poem does not pose a threat to security."

Cold War relic

The Cold War – and, in this instance, the Korean War that raged throughout the peninsula from 1950 to 1953 – cast a long shadow over this ruling. The National Security Act, established in 1948, was created in response to the existential threat posed by communism, embodied by the fledgling North Korean state, and was designed to protect against alleged subversion and infiltration.

The scope of the act extends beyond

The act has a long history of being misapplied for political aims

espionage. According to Article 7, people can be sentenced to up to seven years in prison for "praising", "inciting" or "propagating" the actions of an "anti-government organisation". This behaviour includes the manufacturing, importation, reproduction, possession, distribution or sale of "any [related] documents, drawings or other expression materials". The term "anti-government organisation" is not explicitly defined, creating a vast legal

ABOVE: The scene at Unification Bridge, which has separated the two Koreas since the Korean War

grey area, ripe for potential misuse.

Not that the complexity of South Korea's security landscape can be overlooked, as evidenced by decades of threats and provocations. In 1968, a North Korean commando team infiltrated Seoul, only just failing to assassinate president Park Chung-hee. In 1987, a bomb was planted by North Korean

agents aboard a Korean Air passenger jet, killing 115 people. And in 2010, North Korea shelled Yeonpyeong Island, killing two South Korean civilians.

More recently, North Korea's advances in nuclear and missile programmes, coupled with cyberattacks, have increased the potential of escalation, emphasising the need for laws protecting South Korea's security.

But throughout its history, the application of the National Security Act has varied widely.

For example, in 2011, a court ruled that a man was guilty of violating the act for selling books related to North Korea and Marxism, despite the fact that such works were available to the public elsewhere. In 2012, a man received a suspended prison sentence for retweeting a North Korean account and satirising their propaganda (he was eventually acquitted). In 2015, a Korean-American woman was deported from South Korea for saying complimentary things about North Korea – a move denounced by NGOs and the US government. And in 2021, the South Korean publisher of a memoir of former North Korean leader Kim Il-sung was raided by police, and the book was removed from bookstore shelves.

The "anti-state" threat
The current Yoon Suk Yeol administration seems to be adopting a far-right rhetoric reminiscent of the Donald Trump playbook to rally his conservative supporters, stoking fears of ideological polarisation. Yoon has aggressively targeted the media, labelling it as the purveyor of "fake news", and revoked press credentials of those →

RIGHT: South Korean President Yoon Suk Yeol

→ critical of the government. There has been a surge in defamation cases against the media under his leadership.

Against this backdrop, Yoon and the ruling People Power Party have used the perceived communist threat as a weapon to target political opponents and groups that the government does not favour.

In his August 2023 Liberation Day speech, Yoon referred to his domestic critics as "anti-state forces that blindly follow communist totalitarianism", saying that they "disguised themselves as democracy activists, human rights advocates or progressive activists" – without further elaboration.

In September, Yoon branded those who opposed Seoul's deepening ties with Japan and the USA as "communist totalitarian and anti-state forces", a veiled jab at his opponents including the main opposition Democratic Party.

In October, the then leader of the People Power Party, Kim Gi-hyeon, suggested that North Korea was behind the campaign for accountability by parents of the victims of the deadly 2022 crowd crush in Seoul, which killed 159 people.

The rhetoric is stirring action, and not just against poets. This January, the National Intelligence Service (NIS) and the police raided the Korean Confederation of Trade Unions, alleging that some of its members had violated the National Security Act. The move raised concerns that the allegations were a politicised pretext to target unions.

Even before recent events, the act has a long history of being misapplied for political aims under the guise of countering a fictitious North Korean threat. Over several decades, South Korean authorities have arrested numerous people on charges of spying for North Korea, only to see them exonerated, but often after they have endured lengthy prison sentences.

In 2013, one particularly egregious and high-profile case involved Yu Woo-sung, a North Korean defector who was charged with violating the National Security Act while working as a civil servant in Seoul. He faced accusations of being a spy, orchestrated by the NIS through fabricated evidence. Yoo was eventually found innocent, and employees of the NIS and prosecutors involved in the forgery were punished.

NSA here to stay

The UN has expressed concern on multiple occasions regarding the application of the National Security Act, and Article 7 in particular. Prominent rights groups have advocated for substantial amendments or outright abolition of the law to bring it in line with established international legal standards. South Korea's human rights watchdog recently called Article 7 unconstitutional and has advocated for the law to be abolished completely.

But such calls to abolish it fall on deaf ears. In October 2023, the government asserted that Article 7 was necessary for protecting national security. The government told the UN human rights committee that its actions were geared towards safeguarding freedom of expression for its citizens.

In a move that would have reflected a potential shift in attitudes, in 2022 the South Korean government announced plans to increase public access to North Korean media. However, it was recently reported that the plans had been halted.

Perhaps the starkest of contradictions can be found in the constitution, and the court that governs it. In September 2023, it ruled for the eighth time that the National Security Act was constitutional, suggesting that the law was here to stay in its full current form. Article 37 of the constitution states that "freedoms and rights of citizens may be restricted … only when necessary for national security".

On the same day, the court made another judgment: that a ban on criticising the North Korean regime through leaflet campaigns was not constitutional, citing that it excessively infringed upon freedom of expression. This long-standing practice, which involves sending balloons carrying leaflets critical of the North Korean regime across the border, was prohibited under the previous Moon Jae-in government, and people were charged for defying the ban. Two proposals to revise the law and officially lift the ban on leaflet campaigns are currently under review by the National Assembly.

In South Korea, people have freedom of expression, but only as long as it adheres to the quite literal political correctness of the day. ✖

Raphael Rashid is a freelance journalist based in South Korea

The law, when it suits him

Donald Trump believes in First Amendment rights for himself but not for others. He believes in due process unless it concerns him. **JP O'MALLEY** talks to lawyer **TRISTAN SNELL** about whether his hypocrisy might finally catch up with him

DONALD TRUMP IS the first former president in US history to face criminal charges. Can he be brought to justice?

"I think it's highly likely that Trump is going to be spending the rest of his life in prison," Tristan Snell said from his home in New York.

"A conviction will probably happen by early May and then Trump will be sentenced by August, before we get down to the home stretch of the election season."

The lawyer and media legal commentator was previously assistant attorney-general for the state of New York. With a following of nearly half a million people on X/Twitter, Snell regularly offers his opinion on legal matters. And now his attention is focused on Trump, who's looking to make a quick return to the White House later this year.

Snell recently published Taking Down Trump, a book that outlines "12 rules" for prosecuting Trump, who faces multiple lawsuits and criminal cases, both federally and in a number of states – even while being the Republican party candidate for the 2024 presidential election.

In February, Trump filed an application at the US Supreme Court to keep a federal election interference case on hold while he appeals a lower court's ruling that he is not immune from prosecution. Trump's lawyers have claimed the case threatens the First Amendment rights of Trump, his supporters and volunteers, and all US voters. (The First Amendment of the US Constitution guarantees free speech, a free press and the right to assembly.)

Snell said Trump was cynically attempting to "try and convince a lot of Americans that he is the one who is the guardian of democracy and the rule of law", when in fact Trump had spent decades "believing he was untouchable, invincible and had carte blanche to float above the law".

Snell points to an early Trump tangle with the government, in 1973, when federal prosecutors filed a civil suit against him and his father, Fred, for allegedly discriminating against Black prospective tenants in New York in violation of the Fair Housing Act (charges that Trump to this day denies). The Trumps, represented by notorious lawyer Roy Cohn, responded by filing a lawsuit against the government for $100 million (the equivalent of more than $500 million today). After nearly two years of delays, the case ultimately resulted in a relative slap on the wrist for the Trumps.

"That case established Donald Trump's reputation as someone that you didn't fuck around," said Snell. "The Cohn legal playbook was always: delay, divert, destroy. It was, like, 'Whatever you do to me, I'm going to come back and do to you 10 times worse'."

He added: "Through campaign contributions or charitable donations, or the promise of cheques, Trump always tried to buy off or cosy up to whoever was the elected prosecutor, so they could come to an understanding."

Fast-forward to today and, as we saw during his four years in power, which were defined by regular attacks of the media, Trump has become even more brazen.

Some of the current charges against Trump relate to his actions before and during the riot at the US Capitol in Washington, DC, on 6 January 2021. Others relate to the misuse of classified information. Jack Smith, a special counsel in the Justice Department, has charged Trump with 37 felonies in connection with his removal of documents when he left office in January 2021. The case has been scheduled to go to trial in May.

Snell refers to evidence published by CNN and The New York Times last summer in which Trump was heard on an audio recording at his golf club in New Jersey, in July 2021, openly boasting about a classified military plan for a US attack on Iran. When the tape is played before a jury at trial, it will be extremely difficult for Trump to get out from under it, Snell reckons.

"This recording completely destroys Trump's attempted defence that he didn't know the documents were classified," he said. "It also establishes that Trump had the criminal intent required by the Espionage Act for the wilful retention of defence-related documents.

"In this case, there is also the possibility that there will be security camera footage, where Trump and people in his inner circle are on camera actually moving the documents around or rifling through them. If that evidence →

 **That case established Donald Trump's reputation as someone that you didn't fuck around**

ABOVE: Donald Trump speaks before entering a courtroom at Manhattan criminal court, February 2024

→ is [shown] to exist then it will become clear that Trump was trying to delete the security cam footage as best he could. Then we have a Nixon-Watergate situation, except that it's multiplied by 10."

Smith has also charged Trump with four federal felonies in connection with his attempt to remain in power as president after losing the 2020 election. Snell believes this case – which is scheduled to begin in March – is the most serious one Trump faces. "The case is moving very fast, so there is not as much room for Trump to delay it," he explained.

One of the great unknowns is whether Trump – if he is elected president again in November – will try to pardon himself of any federal

> Many of New York's top legal minds over the years have looked the other way because Trump gave generously

Fulton County, Georgia, has brought a racketeering case against Trump and 18 others, alleging they tried to steal the last presidential election. That case is scheduled to begin this August. A bigger case with more defendants, it's going to be more logistically complex to bring to trial, according to Snell. But it is a case brought by a state prosecutor rather than by the federal government, and that has implications when it comes to presidential pardons.

"If Trump becomes president [in November] and this case results in a conviction, Trump cannot pardon himself for state crimes," he said.

This January, Trump appeared in court several times. One of those appearances was in a civil fraud trial, led by New York attorney-general Letitia James, who has sued Trump and accused him and his family of committing financial fraud to gain better credit ratings.

Another of his January court appearances resulted in him being ordered to pay $83.3 million to writer E Jean Carroll for defamation. It followed a previous award of $5 million to Carroll after Trump was found liable last year for sexually abusing and defaming her.

An earlier case Snell worked on involved Trump's previously largest legal financial settlement, and the lawyer examines the finer details of that case in Taking Down Trump. That investigation began in 2011 when Snell began working with a team of lawyers employed with the New York attorney-general's office. Together, they built a civil prosecution against Trump, which they filed in 2013 and won. The case resulted in a $25 million settlement to former students at Trump University.

Founded in 2005 and in existence until 2010, the fake training college offered its "students" the chance to gain knowledge in real-estate dealmaking. Participants paid an average of about $35,000 for fake diplomas, and Trump personally pocketed $42 million from the sham education programme. Snell said the outcome of the case was notable because "before this case, whenever Trump went up against people in court, he usually bulldozed them".

Trump has navigated the legal system for decades through political favours and dodgy financial donations, believes the lawyer. Snell points out that many of New York's top legal minds have looked the other way because Trump gave generously to their favourite charities.

"But the days when Trump could just go and scare – or buy off – a prosecutor are well and truly over. These are very serious offences with which Trump is charged," he added.

At the same time Snell warned that Trump's various trials over the coming weeks and months were not a slam dunk on the side of justice, and if the former president were elected to the White House in November, an extremist agenda "to destroy the American Republic and the Constitution" could prevail.

If Trump manages to become president again, "it's going to show how he has convinced, conned and fooled a majority of the country that he does believe in the rule of law and equal justice, and that is very problematic".

He added: "Trump is on trial many times in the months to come, but it is really a trial for the soul of the American Republic." ✖

JP O'Malley is a freelance journalist

convictions he might have received by then. If he did try to pardon himself, he would be in legally uncharted waters and it's unclear if he would be successful.

There is one case in which he would definitely not be able to pull it off. Fani Willis, a district attorney in

'An extraordinary novel. Truly important'
WILLIAM BOYD

'Lai Wen is a brilliant storyteller'
XINRAN

Publishing for the 35th anniversary of Tiananmen Square

JUNE 2024

Swift

SPECIAL REPORT

"Komar did not dream that her actions would mean the embassy would essentially refuse her a new passport"

REFUSED A PASSPORT | SALLY GIMSON | P.66

Nowhere is safe

Autocracies have always gone after their critics. But new technology and global dynamics have made the situation far worse for those living overseas, writes **ALEXANDER DUKALSKIS**

IN JANUARY, THE US Department of Justice charged two Canadian nationals for participating in a murder-for-hire plot in Maryland in late 2020 and early 2021. One of the men, a member of the Hells Angels Motorcycle Club, contacted the other and they planned to assemble a team to perpetrate the murder. The fee was to be $350,000 plus $20,000 in expenses. The twist is that the hitmen were hired by an Iranian drug lord with ties to that country's intelligence community, and the target was an unnamed Iranian defector living in Maryland. The charging documents indicate that the murder was meant to be gruesome to act as an example to other defectors.

This episode is only the most recent high-profile form of transnational repression – states coercing their citizens while they are abroad. Most state repression takes place within a country's own territorial jurisdiction, with governments banning civil society groups, jailing members of the opposition on spurious grounds, violently cracking down on protests, harassing and threatening critics – both online and offline – and myriad other tactics.

Repression is far from new – in fact it is an ancient technology of political order. But TR has entered the public consciousness in a pronounced way only recently. In the last few years, it has been the subject of editorials, columns and coverage in major media outlets such as The Washington Post, Time and The Guardian. Freedom House, the US-based advocacy organisation, has devoted significant time and resources to produce reports and analysis on the topic.

The result of this attention is that a bill currently in the US Congress, the Transnational Repression Policy Act, would require the president to penalise perpetrators of TR and the US State Department to devise a TR strategy, and mandate training for some law enforcement agencies. The Joe Biden administration has announced new executive branch programmes to reduce TR, and various European bodies have also begun to pay attention to the issue, with an international declaration setting out principles for combatting it.

Given the recent attention, one might be forgiven for thinking that TR is new. But it is not. Chinese revolutionary Sun Yat-sen was kidnapped in London in 1896 and taken to the Chinese embassy, where he was held for 12 days and released only following a public outcry. Russian revolutionary Leon Trotsky was murdered by a secret agent of the NKVD in Mexico in 1940, and during the 1970s Operation Condor saw South American dictatorships co-operating to repress each other's dissidents. Iranian authorities were targeting dissidents in Maryland as far back as 1980.

But TR is newly salient. Why? The proximate cause is the grisly 2018 murder of Saudi journalist-in-exile Jamal Khashoggi. He was a well-connected figure in political and journalistic circles so his shocking murder by Saudi agents in Istanbul was bound to attract attention. For many, his assassination put a face to a practice that had long been perpetrated by autocrats.

A more general underlying cause of it becoming more well-known is the revival of authoritarian rule globally. Political scientists debate the nature and extent of global democratic backsliding, but this much is clear: the international environment is much friendlier to authoritarian governments now than it was 30 years ago. Many authoritarian states are acting with newfound confidence abroad while some important democracies are challenged from within by illiberal movements.

This is important because authoritarian states – non-democracies – are much more likely to perpetrate TR. Democracies have internal mechanisms for people to express their dissent, and liberal democracies tolerate a wide range of political speech and activism, meaning that they generate fewer political exiles in the first place. Even when people do feel compelled to leave, the laws and norms of democracy restrain their governments more than their authoritarian counterparts. There are exceptions and grey areas, of course, but in general TR is perpetrated by authoritarian regimes.

The rise of China as a global power shapes the international environment in even more authoritarian-friendly ways, advancing norms hostile to state accountability for human rights violations – particularly when it comes to civil and political rights. When other authoritarian states come in for criticism by transnational human rights groups or liberal democratic states, China can act as a powerful protector.

Given that it is hostile to dissent at home, it is perhaps no surprise that China is a major perpetrator of TR. The

During the 1970s Operation Condor saw South American dictatorships co-operating to repress each other's dissidents

signal couldn't be clearer: so long as TR does not impinge on Chinese interests or sovereignty, other authoritarian governments won't get pushback from Beijing if they want to hunt down dissidents abroad. And it is even better if states co-operate in the repatriation of Chinese exiles.

But it's not just great powers such as China that engage in TR. Given its small size and relatively short global reach, Rwanda is a prolific transnational repressor. President Paul Kagame has run the country for decades by securing electoral majorities of more than 90% in heavily rigged affairs. Not only are internal detractors and opposition members silenced, over the years his rivals and critics have turned up murdered in Kenya, South Africa and Uganda. Kagame has always denied any involvement but he has cheered on the assassinations, saying in 2014: "Any person still alive who may be plotting against Rwanda, whoever they are, will pay the price… Whoever it is, it is a matter of time."

And although TR is not new, globalisation and technology facilitates new forms. Social media apps such as China's WeChat not only link the Chinese diaspora to Beijing's propaganda streams and censorship practices, they also help facilitate TR through messaging and surveillance. Relatives of people living abroad can be pressured to contact their loved ones to implore them to cease their activism in exchange for their family being spared repression at home.

The Iranian murder-for-hire plot in Maryland was organised through an encrypted messaging app.

When a case is brought to light, authoritarian governments can confuse public discussion by social media trolling and astroturfing (presenting an orchestrated campaign in the guise of comments from the public). Ultimately, while the underlying logistics of information manipulation and sending threatening communications

to dissidents abroad are not new, technology makes it cheaper, easier and almost instantaneous.

Another distinctive feature of contemporary globalisation is widespread international student mobility. Students away from their home country may learn fresh perspectives on its politics, or even become involved in activism and student groups. This is a normal part of studying abroad and broadening one's intellectual horizons, but authoritarian states wish to inoculate their students from influences that may challenge their governments. Sometimes, as a recent Freedom House report shows, this involves TR in the form of harassment and intimidation by embassy officials or proxy student groups.

Political science researchers are mapping the patterns of TR, recently discovering that in autocratic "host" states TR perpetrators rely on co-operation from their fellow autocrats, whereas in democratic ones the perpetrators opt for direct attacks that circumvent the host states. The Iran-Hells Angel co-operation is an example of the latter.

In a new paper, The Long Arm and the Iron Fist: Authoritarian Crackdowns and Transnational Repression, my co-authors and I have found that TR tends to follow on from domestic crackdowns as opposition and witnesses flee abroad.

Much work remains to be done, but what is clear is that authoritarian states wish to control threats in the international environment. They'll continue to do so, and democracies have to be prepared to adapt. ✖

Alexander Dukalskis is an associate professor at University College Dublin and a contributor to a forthcoming book on transnational repression

Welcome to the dictators' playground

Turkey has become an unofficial HQ for authoritarian regimes around the world. **KAYA GENÇ** explores why

SPECIAL REPORT

THIS OCTOBER WILL mark the sixth anniversary of Jamal Khashoggi's murder in Turkey. On 2 October 2018 a team of agents dispatched by the Saudi government strangled the dissident Washington Post columnist after he entered the consulate building in Istanbul. The respected journalist's body was dismembered and, according to Turkish intelligence, dissolved in acid. The CIA said Khashoggi's state-employed assassins acted at the behest of Saudi Crown Prince Mohammed bin Salman.

Since that dark day, Turkey's reputation as a hub of transnational repression has grown.

Uyghur dissidents in the country are one group feeling the effects of China's transnational power. Turkey was once seen as a haven for the persecuted people from China's northwest given the linguistic, cultural and religious overlaps, and was therefore home to the largest numbers of Uyghurs outside of China. Now the incidents of attacks of Uyghur dissidents are going up and up. According to a 2023 report from Safeguard Defenders, more than one-third of Uyghurs interviewed in Turkey said they had been harassed by Chinese police or state agents while in the country. Leading activists have been deported. It's unclear about Turkey's stance here and they have yet to ratify an extradition treaty which Beijing signed in December 2020. Still, it's far from safe and if Turkey do ratify the treaty Uyghurs will be even more exposed.

Another group to feel the effects are Iranian dissidents. Over the past half-decade, Iranian intelligence agents have carried out multiple operations on Turkish soil, at times even aided by members of Turkey's judiciary and police force.

In September 2023, a former Turkish prosecutor was sentenced to 11 years and eight months in jail for collaborating with Iranian intelligence. Among the 15 others tried in court were two police officers. In 2019, the prosecutor allegedly took $50,000 in return for providing the location of Mohammed Rezaei, a former Iranian navy officer, to Iranian intelligence.

The operation to kidnap Rezaei (conducted using the car of the Turkish state prosecutor) failed. The attempt to capture Shahnam Golshani, the manager of the Iranian website Mesghal, also failed. An authority on the value of hard currency, Golshani's website was blocked in Iran in 2013 after president Mahmoud Ahmadinejad lost control of the currency market and asked Golshani to publish lower rates for hard currency to calm people, which he refused to do. There were reports that the Courts of First Instance issued the death penalty against Golshani. He fled the country illegally over the border into Turkey in 2013.

Iranian intelligence failed to capture Golshani and Rezaei but managed to abduct a former Iranian colonel, Mashali Firouze. Another "success" came in 2022, when the Iranian dissident Mohammad Bagher Moradi, nine years after taking refuge in Turkey, left home to buy bread. He never returned. The police found his abandoned car, and his family pointed to the Iranian intelligence as culprits. Moradi, a member of Saraye Ahl-e Ghalam (Writers' Association), had received a five-year prison sentence on the charge of "illegal gathering and collusion against national security" while living in Iran.

Esmaeil Fattahi, a dissident on the watchlist of Iranian intelligence, said he can't ignore these developments and just continue with his life. Born in 1988, Fattahi has been living in Turkey since 2015. His crime was to blog about the political situation in Iran. He was part of a group that worked clandestinely, distributing pamphlets, conducting secret meetings and putting up graffiti to highlight human rights and women's rights struggles inside Iranian factories. →

LEFT: Taksim Square in central Istanbul. The city has become a haven for political dissidents fleeing persecution but it's far from safe

→ First arrested aged 15 in Tabriz, where he lived, Fattahi spent six months in prison. Four years later, he was again sentenced to six months. His arrest in 2010 led to a five-year prison term. By the time of his release, Fattahi became convinced he'd leave Iran. "When I left prison in 2015, I was 27, and I had spent around a fourth of [my life], six years, in prison," he told Index.

After his release, Fattahi learned another case had been opened against him – for reporting on the torturous conditions in Iran's prisons to international human rights organisations. Also, he couldn't get employment.

"The Iranian media called me 'the dog of Israel and America' and claimed I was an agent, a communist," he recalled. The owner of a cafe where he worked offered his apologies before firing Fattahi. "Once they learned who I was, it was over. Nobody wanted to take the risk."

Fattahi made headlines in Turkey when, in 2021, he was arrested with three other Iranian dissidents in the Anatolian city of Denizli for attending a protest event against Turkey's withdrawal from the Istanbul Convention. This Council of Europe treaty, which Turkey had been the first to sign in 2011, opposes violence against women and domestic violence. But as Turkish strongman Recep Tayyip Erdoğan and his far-right allies launched a war against the idea of a culturally determined gender, they turned the treaty into a hate object which they claim is defended by woke race traitors, and nefarious powers in the pay of George Soros.

Fattahi joined Leili Faraji and Zeinab Sahafi for the protest, took a banner and delivered a speech. He was joined by members of the Iranian LGBTQI community in Turkey. A month later, he received a call from the mother of Sahafi, who said her daughter was detained. Two other phone calls followed. An ally, Mohammad Pourakbari Kermani, who hadn't even participated in the protest, was also detained.

Fattahi didn't return home and headed to the police headquarters in Denizli, where he was swiftly put behind bars. The four dissidents refused to sign a voluntary return document and spent a month in a deportation centre in Aydın. Public furore and a viral social media campaign followed. Amnesty and Freedom House pressured Turkey's Interior Ministry. There was even a parliamentary question about the arrests. "We got out thanks to those," said Fattahi.

Nowadays he lives in a different Anatolian town. "Iran is a totalitarian state with not a shred of democracy, press freedom or freedom of expression," he said. "Here in Turkey,

ABOVE: A Turkish policeman heads towards Saudi Arabia's Consul General's residence in Istanbul on 17 October 2018 to collect evidence over the disappearance of the Saudi journalist Jamal Khashoggi, who was later confirmed murdered

police can detain you for your political views and a judge can, at most, sentence you to prison. In Iran, they hang you or subject you to whipping."

He is worried about being kidnapped. "For years, Iranian agents entered Turkey easily. Last year, a friend of ours was assassinated in Istanbul," he said. The situation is particularly perilous in cities such as Van, close to the Iranian border. "Iranian agents tried to kidnap a friend of mine to Iran last month."

Fattahi receives death threats on social media all the time, and reads emails whose senders describe what they'll "do" to him "soon".

"I've been getting those for the past seven years. I can't just ignore them," he said.

Still, he feels lucky. Many refugees live in abject poverty in Turkey, with no financial support and no work permits, which leads them to work illegally. Undocumented refugees do the most challenging work for the longest hours and receive the lowest wages. As a freelancer working from home, Fattahi can at least organise his life.

"I order all my food and groceries from my phone. I try not to go out at all. I only go out to walk my dog, which I do very carefully. Most refugees work 12 hours outside, and many have committed suicide because of the conditions."

Last year, a friend of Fattahi, who had been in Turkey for seven years, called him to say he was going back. "I encountered so much racism here, and my wife left me because of our financial situation. I prefer going to prison in Iran than being here," Fattahi remembered him saying.

In 2019, the police broke down the door of Fattahi's house, and he woke up with a gun next to his head. Four men in black balaclavas took him to the police headquarters.

"There were cameras in the station, so they beat me up in the toilet," Fattahi said. The following day, they set him free. When he sued the police who intimidated him, a court handed him a seven-month prison sentence and a fine for "resisting security forces".

Pondering the future, he is particularly worried about kidnapping attempts conducted by Iranian spies who can then return to Iran without any hurdles. "I have to be constantly careful about my relationships here," he said.

Dissidents from other countries, such as Eva Rapoport, who is Russian, encounter different challenges. The cultural anthropologist and photographer left Russia in 2013 before the annexation of Crimea. "I thought that the situation would keep deteriorating and one day all would go down in flames," she recalled. Rapoport moved from Moscow to Southeast Asia and lived in Indonesia for a while before ending up in Turkey in 2020.

She rented an apartment in Istanbul, hoping things would return to normal. But they went in the opposite direction. The new anti-war wave of Russian immigration began, with thousands of liberal Russians and those opposed to the war moving to Turkey.

Rapoport noticed she had advantages compared with people who had left Russia without any preparation. "I had local knowledge about how to live in Istanbul," she said. She decided to put that to good use.

Rapoport is part of the Ark Project, founded in March 2022 as a response to the criminalisation of Russians who disagree with the war in Ukraine. "The Ark is the first initiative that centrally helps people from Russia who left because of an anti-war stance," its website announces. "Now, the audience of the Ark is about half a million people."

It had been straightforward for Russians to go to Turkey, a popular tourist destination since the 1990s. For years, scores of Russians came to the Mediterranean haven of Antalya and stayed in all-inclusive hotels. "For dissidents who take refuge in Turkey, they don't feel threatened, and here they don't feel like aliens," Rapoport said.

She had spent months organising

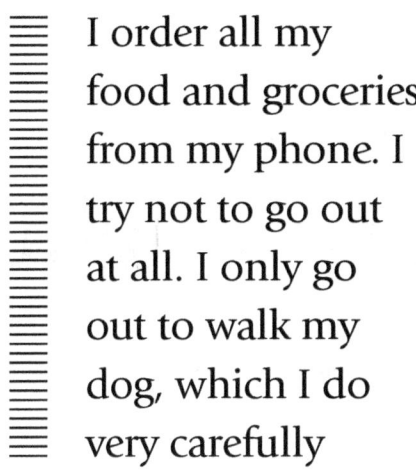

I order all my food and groceries from my phone. I try not to go out at all. I only go out to walk my dog, which I do very carefully

lectures on topics pertaining to the situation in Russia but also addressing Turkish and Middle Eastern history, culture and politics. The programme – for which she selected speakers from September 2022 until March 2023 – did very well. "Our most popular events were gathering over 100 people. We had one poetry reading in November which attracted 60 people." But in December 2022, things took a turn for the worse.

"Turkish authorities stopped issuing residency permits. People began getting rejections. Nobody knew what was happening. By spring, lots of people who were going to stay left," Rapoport said. Their depature was not voluntarily. Instead they were pushed out, their visas not renewed.

There are various theories about why: some link it to pressure from Putin, a strong ally of Erdoğan, not to provide refuge to dissidents, but it's equally possible to explain Erdoğan's change of heart as the result of the rise of anti-refugee sentiment among the electorate.

Like Fattahi, Rapoport is concerned about the future of dissidents here. "I don't see my future even for the next 10 months in Turkey," she said. "I was quite enthusiastic here when the immigration began, right after the war and the first wave, and the second one in September, following mobilisation. There was this feeling that Istanbul could become a new hub for Russian opposition culture, a good version of what Russian cultural and intellectual life could be. Then it became clear that people were not staying; people who were eager to start some projects here or had started businesses also didn't have their residencies renewed. People left, and they will keep leaving."

The Ark Project, which conducts its communications via Telegram, has thousands of members in Turkey. Is Rapoport aware of the fate they share with Iranian dissidents?

"There were jokes here about Russians and Iranians coming together and having an argument about whose passport is worse," she said.

Even as Russia falls under more international sanctions, Iranian passports are still worse in terms of the number of countries its holders can travel to, she added.

Both Fattahi and Rapoport say their main problem is not knowing what the future holds.

"I have no idea whether I'll leave Turkey next year or in a decade. I can neither study, open a new business or set up a life," Fattahi said. "I'm 35, and I have spent almost a decade here, not going to college and amassing nothing to secure my life. If I left Turkey today, I'd begin from scratch."

Like Rapoport, Fattahi had tried to initiate cultural events for like-minded Iranian dissidents. He rented a cafe where they could read books together and have weekly screenings of films about social issues, including LGBTQI rights. "But we can't do those now," he said. "People in Iran think Turkey is a free country with freedom for women and the freedom to consume alcohol. They don't realise Turkey is not a free and democratic country until they start living here." ✖

Kaya Genç is Index's Turkey contributing editor

The overseas repressors who are evading the spotlight

Central Asian governments go after dissidents abroad with little fear of repercussion, making them some of the most ruthless international players around, writes **EMILY COUCH**

IN THE JOURNALISTIC and policy spheres, Central Asia – a vast region encompassing Kazakhstan, Kyrgyzstan, Uzbekistan, Tajikistan and Turkmenistan – is often simplistically (and lazily) described as being stuck between two great powers: Russia to the north and China to the east.

The authoritarianism of these behemoth neighbours means Central Asian regimes do not receive the international attention they warrant – and this is particularly true when it comes to transnational repression. According to last year's report Still Not Safe: Transnational Repression in 2022, published by US-based human rights organisation Freedom House, Tajikistan, Turkmenistan and Uzbekistan rank alongside Russia and China as the most prolific perpetrators of transnational repression.

Despite occasional political openings, authoritarian tendencies continue to plague the nations of Central Asia. Tajikistan and Turkmenistan are both considered "Not free", according to Freedom House's Freedom in the World index, scoring just 7/100 and 2/100 respectively. While Kyrgyzstan ranks higher, the government of president Sadyr Japarov has increasingly eroded democratic freedoms. The security services of these countries – who are the direct implementers of transnational repression – represent the worst of these repressive tendencies.

"There was never really any reform of the security services after the Soviet collapse," said Steve Swerdlow, an associate professor of the practice of human rights at the University of Southern California, who specialises in Central Asia. "There has never been a rupture with KGB culture. There has been no truth and reconciliation, no opening up."

Index has spoken to three activists who live in the shadow of transnational repression. Farhod Odinaev and Fatima (a pseudonym) are from Tajikistan, the Central Asian country responsible for the highest number of transnational cases. Odinaev is a member of the banned Islamic Renaissance Party, which opposes the regime of President Emomali Rahmon, and founder of an independent TV channel based in Moscow. Fatima is a journalist and researcher focusing on social issues and press freedom in Central Asia.

Leila Nazgul Seiitbek is a lawyer and human rights activist from

> **Authoritarian tendencies continue to plague the nations of Central Asia**

Kyrgyzstan who came under fire from the government after uncovering a land corruption scheme in the country's Chui region.

All now live outside their countries of origin, yet continue to face varying

SPECIAL REPORT

PICTURED: Left to right: Uzbek President Shavkat Mirziyoyev, Tajik President Emomali Rahmon, Kazakh President Kassym-Jomart Tokayev, US President Joe Biden, Kyrgyz President Sadyr Zhaparov and Turkmen President Serdar Berdymukhamedov at the UN in September 2023

degrees of intimidation because of their professional and political activities. Their experiences illuminate the commonalities in the repressive tactics used by Central Asian governments, as well as the immense toll that these can take on those who dare to speak out.

Targeting activists' families who remain in the country is standard modus operandi for these repressive regimes. The Tajik government went after Odinaev's father, mother and brother.

"Once the security services learned that I was the head of the TV station, they began persecuting my family ... They called in my father for questioning ... then they called in my brother," he told Index.

→

INDEXONCENSORSHIP.ORG **59**

> Targeting activists' family members who remain in the country is standard modus operandi for these repressive regimes

→ "They brought my mother and sister in for interrogation and subjected them to severe intimidation and threats. They threatened to rape my sister and her son who was just 19 at the time."

While her family has not experienced such harsh treatment, Fatima told Index that her mother had received calls from the security services demanding that she tell Fatima to stop speaking and writing publicly.

The nature of transnational repression means that the victims of its most severe manifestations cannot share their experiences because they are unjustly imprisoned, scared into silence through physical attacks, or murdered. Odinaev, Fatima and Seiitbek live with the constant anxiety that they could be next.

In March 2020, Tajik activist Ilhomjon Yakubov was beaten by two men in the Lithuanian capital of Vilnius. Odinaev said: "There has always been the feeling that they could arrest me again or that the German authorities could deport me because I do not yet have refugee status, or that they could attack me on the street like they did to Ilhomjon Yakubov."

Seiitbek reports having received graphic threats of violence over Facebook for her activism, and she told Index of her fear of deportation. "I don't travel to countries that may be willing to hand me over to any of the post-Soviet states that are looking to have me imprisoned," she said.

Deportation is also a constant worry for Fatima, who had an anxiety-inducing experience at Istanbul airport last December. "I was detained for two hours, with my phone and passport taken away, and questioned about my travels. My heart sank, [and I thought] 'This is it, I am getting arrested and deported to Tajikistan because of what I do'." The detention turned out to be a routine check and she was released.

Odinaev, Fatima and Seiitbek all speak of the psychological toll. "As a man it is difficult for me to admit that I'm afraid but these thoughts sometimes come to me," said Odinaev. Seiitbek describes having "just no will to live" after she claimed asylum in Austria in 2016. For Fatima, it is "constant anxiety for me and my mum".

To avoid the worst fates of dissidents, Odinaev, Fatima and Seiitbek have all engaged in self-censorship. "After [the Tajik authorities] designated me as a 'terrorist', I no longer expressed my opinion on social media, I no longer gave interviews," said Odinaev. "It was this way until I left Russia for the EU in 2020."

Seiitbek reports a similar experience, telling Index that she "kept silent for several years" until Austria granted her asylum.

As someone who regularly writes and comments for international and regionally-focused outlets, Fatima treads a difficult line between continuing to share her expertise and keeping herself and her family safe. "I do not touch certain topics, like the president and the people connected to him," she said. "If I do end up covering a risky subject, I do not use a byline. If I am asked for a quote or for background information for a piece about Tajikistan, I ask to stay anonymous."

Central Asian activists find themselves largely undefended by the international community. Odinaev said the international response had been woefully inadequate. "I have not seen any action from international institutions except for human rights organisations that put out statements," he said. "Tajik officials and security services feel very comfortable, they travel all around the world, they work with all governments, there is no danger to them [...] so year after year they continue to persecute political activists."

Seiitbek expands on this issue, stating that while the Magnitsky Act allows the USA and its allies to sanction the perpetrators of transnational repression, it has not, thus far, been used for this purpose. This, she says, needs to change. "Sanctioning human rights abusers would send a strong signal to authorities that democratic countries will not tolerate this behaviour."

The arms of Dushanbe, Bishkek and Tashkent are just as long and – in many cases – just as dangerous as those of Moscow and Beijing. Since 1991, the West has too often made the mistake of viewing the region either as "Putin's backyard" or as an arena for "great power competition" between Russia and China.

This view of Central Asia makes it easy for the authoritarianism of its governments to be overlooked or dismissed as somehow being less severe than that of its larger neighbours. Until the West devotes greater resources to understanding and engaging with Central Asian countries on their own terms, activists and journalists such as Odinaev, Fatima and Seiitbek will remain at risk.

Central Asian activists abroad will keep speaking out for democracy and human rights despite the danger they face. Odinaev sums up how many Central Asian activists cope: "The feeling of fear is always with you ... but this is life. You have to live somehow." ✖

Emily Couch is a contributing editor for Index, reporting on Ukraine, Russia and Central Asia

SPECIAL REPORT

Everything everywhere all at once

Digital advances have destroyed the ability of dissidents to live an anonymous life, writes **DAISY RUDDOCK**

WHEN ASKED ABOUT their countries' experiences with transnational repression, representatives of NGOs from Saudi Arabia, Lebanon and China painted a bleak picture. Responding to a recent Index survey all confirmed the worst – that it had typically escalated or at best plateaued over the last few years. The primary reason? Online.

Social media allows an unprecedented level of access to people and a forum to harass in a way that was unthinkable a few decades ago. Meanwhile, digital tools, especially spyware, erode the safety and security surrounding one's whereabouts, one's contacts, even one's bank details. It is no longer enough to put physical distance between person and state when the long arm of the state can slide into your DMs.

This was something an organisation working on China said had become particularly pronounced recently. They wished to remain anonymous though and in this day and age who can blame them?

Of course, transnational repression remains a significant issue outside of the digital sphere. Another tactic identified by each survey respondent as common was the harassment of family members within the country. This has long been a tool of authoritarian states due to the accessibility of those who remain in the country and the psychological impact it can have.

The European Saudi Organisation for Human Rights (ESOHR), whose representative responded to this survey, have monitored and documented numerous instances where relatives of activists who shed light on human rights violations in the state have been targeted by the Saudi government. Numerous dissenters have seen their family members being arrested and tortured in an attempt to silence them, with many receiving calls from the government urging them to return to Saudi Arabia in exchange for guarantees that their loved ones would not be persecuted or arrested.

In one case identified by the organisation, the brother of political activist Sheikh Hassan Al-Salah was arrested, tortured and kept in solitary confinement just for allegedly making contact with his sibling. Al-Salah himself hasn't seen his son in over six years due to the fear that the same may happen to him.

Respondents to the survey drew on their experience and expertise to suggest ways in which states may be able to tackle the ever-growing problem of transnational repression – something which is urgently needed.

A spokesperson for Social Media Exchange, a Lebanese NGO advocating for digital rights in the Middle East and North Africa region, suggested that access to fair trials should be a priority when attempting to handle issues of transnational repression. They say this will "allow victims to express themselves instead of executing administration decisions by law force without any possible appeal of the decision".

Another suggestion came from Duaa Dhainy, a senior researcher for the ESOHR, who argued that states must take a stand against other states attempting to suppress citizens overseas. Dhainy stated that the impact of transnational repression could be curbed by states "not handing over wanted persons to countries, especially politicians", and stressed the importance of protecting refugees "by all means".

All of these are starts but it's going to take a huge global effort to stop a trend that shows no signs of slowing. ✖

Daisy Ruddock is editorial assistant at Index

53(01):61/61|DOI:10.1177/03064220241243229

RIGHT: According to our survey, digital security was the largest threat to overseas dissidents

A fatal game of international hide and seek

Eritrea's government is reaching across borders to sow discord and silence its critics, **DESSALE BEREKHET** tells **DANSON KAHYANA**

SINCE 1993, WHEN Isaias Afwerki took power in the newly-born Eritrea, the country has remained what the Human Rights Watch World Report of 2023 called "a one-man dictatorship under an unelected president, with no legislature, no independent civil society organisations or media outlets, and no independent judiciary".

Afwerki's rule is characterised by myriad human rights abuses including indefinite military conscription and forced labour, unlawful, prolonged and abusive detentions, enforced disappearances and a clampdown on religious freedom outside the four recognised denominations (Sunni Islam and the Eritrean Orthodox, Roman Catholic and Lutheran churches). Because of these violations, hundreds of thousands of Eritreans have fled the country.

One of those people is Dessale Berekhet, a writer and journalist who now lives in Norway. Among his awards are the PEN Català International Free Voice Prize and the International Press Freedom Award. He's written numerous books, including Zingbaba and the Magic Tree, and in 2014 he helped found Eritrean PEN.

His move to Norway in October 2012 was preceded by two others. He lived in Sudan for the last three months of 2010 and then in Uganda. The circumstances under which he left those two countries for Norway point to the wide reach of Afwerki's repressive apparatus.

Berekhet remembers how astonished he was when a close friend in Sudan turned against him for being critical of Afwerki.

"I could not believe it when he threatened to kill me if I did not cease my critical journalism," he said, shocked that his friend, an educated man, could not see that Afwerki was destroying Eritrea and needed to be exposed as a tyrant and megalomaniac.

"I expected this friend to support my work the way other colleagues were doing [but] his chilling threat to end my life made me realise how people who are close to us – people we consider friends and brothers – can become the regime's tools of transnational repression."

With a group of friends in Eritrea and Uganda, Berekhet started a website – Unitedheartz.com – to continue his work of scrutinising Afwerki's regime, but he was hit by another blow: the man who designed and administrated the website also turned against him. Accusing Berekhet of using the website to discredit the Eritrean government, he blocked him from accessing the domain, bringing the curtain down on the well-read dissident publication which had access to reliable and credible informants within Eritrea and the government itself.

"I could not believe that the person you have contracted to design and build a house for you can throw you out of it because you are using it for a business he does not like," Berekhet said with a wry smile, humour being one of the resources he deploys to remain sane in a world where the people he once trusted as allies have turned out to be a tyrant's accomplices.

With constant threats against his life, it became clear to Berekhet that it was not safe to stay in Uganda. With the help of the International Cities of Refuge Network, he relocated to Norway where he hoped for better security. Shortly after Berekhet left Kampala, a friend

> His chilling threat to end my life made me realise how people who are close to us – people we consider friends and brothers – can become the regime's tools of transnational repression

was beaten by fellow Eritreans, and thankfully survived.

The other tactic the Eritrean government uses to sow mayhem among dissidents beyond its borders is open intimidation. Berekhet has been a victim of this on many occasions.

He has received numerous death threats on social media from Eritreans around the world who accuse him of telling lies against Afwerki and his government. In 2022, someone posted his Norwegian address and phone number on Facebook, with instructions to assassins to silence him forever.

"Of course, this intimidation has not succeeded in frightening me into silence," Berekhet said. "I am aware that it is because of the effectiveness of my critical commentary on the regime that the tyrant and his accomplices wish me dead."

He explained that the government also infiltrates Eritrean asylum and refugee communities in order to sow discord among them. People are often accused of being moles hired by the government to spy on the communities, which has led to open brawls and even deaths.

Disinformation is rife as well and used as a targeting tactic.

"One time, the regime opened so many Facebook accounts in my name, and with images of me as profile pictures, that I myself would take time to tell which one was genuinely mine. Imagine the amount of misinformation and disinformation that was posted out to the public, purportedly from me, portraying me a treasonous fellow and a homosexual, which in Eritrea means a perverted human being, a beast," Berekhet recalled.

And he said journalists faced a different disinformation trap. Somebody in Eritrea could call a dissident journalist, informing them of an important (but false) development back home – say, the death of a high-ranking military officer. Trusting the source, the dissident breaks the news to international audiences, and in the process destroys a career built over decades.

ABOVE AND LEFT: Eritrean writer Dessale Berekhet, who has been attacked across borders

> The regime opened so many Facebook accounts in my name, and with images of me as profile pictures, that I myself would take time to tell which one was genuinely mine

"I personally, while working for the website in Uganda, received such false information. And I broke it as news," Berekhet told Index.

Because of the menace of transnational repression, dissidents live in fear wherever they are living.

"The risk that I could be killed or kidnapped, or members of my family harmed by hired assassins of the state, is ever present," Berekhet said.

But none of this has deterred him. He continues to tell the world about what is happening in Eritrea through journalism, creative writing, interviews and participating at conferences.

"The tyrannical regime in Eritrea thrives on ignorance and fear, so every effort to enlighten the citizens of the country that there are better ways of being governed and that it is possible to rise up against a bad regime and do away with it is important," he said. ✖

Danson Kahyana is a poet, author and scholar at Makerere University and Stellenbosch University and a fellow at the Carr Centre for Human Rights Policy at Harvard Kennedy School. He is Index's contributing editor for East Africa

Our principles are not for sale

A Thai student publisher rejected a lucrative offer to be bought out and shut down by a Chinese businessman. **JIRAPREEYA SAEBOO** discusses the details

RUNNING A PUBLISHING house in Thailand that is dedicated to promoting ideas about democracy, equality and freedom was always going to be risky but we didn't expect attempts to shut us down to come in the form of wealthy Chinese businessmen offering us lots of cash. Still, that's what happened.

In September 2022, Sam Yan Press were approached by a private investigative firm in Thailand, speaking on behalf of a Chinese businessman, who offered us two million *baht* (approximately $55,000) in exchange for shutting down our student-run publishing house and providing official dissolution documentation. The motive behind this perplexing deal was to showcase influence in Thailand and improve relations with the Chinese government before the Chinese Communist Party's annual Congress.

Established in 2017, we are a student-run publishing house. Over the years, we have translated and published books on philosophy, feminism, Thai politics and progressive ideas, including works by well-known Chinese dissidents.

Our venture commenced with our inaugural book dedicated to Joshua Wong, the Hong Kong protest leader, released on his birthday during his incarceration. Subsequent publications include writings by Nobel laureate and human rights activist Liu Xiaobo, who died whilst in custody in China, a prominent book about the Hong Kong protests by the historian Jeffrey Wasserstrom, collected writings of jailed Uyghur freedom fighter Ilham Tohti, a book on Taiwan independence, a memoir of the exiled physicist who stood up against an authoritarian regime, Fang Lizhi, and an upcoming book on Chinese feminist history by the academic Leta Hong Fincher.

In addition to our publications, we actively engage in various movements to promote democracy. We consistently participate in the #MilkTeaAlliance, a pro-democracy movement initiated by activists in Thailand, Hong Kong, Taiwan, Myanmar and Laos, fostering international solidarity and sharing the struggle against dictatorships.

Of course, we were always aware of the risks associated with the nature of our publications, particularly in Thailand, a country that is itself plagued by censorship. Plus there is the threat from China, our "Big Brother" to the north of Thailand, not least because the majority of our works involve criticising the Chinese government.

It was not until our first contact on 5 May 2022 with the Thai agent that we actually experienced pushback. Netiwit Chotiphatphaisal, the founder of Sam Yan Press and a vocal Thai student activist who has been outspoken on Chinese politics, received an email from a private law firm in Thailand. The email stated that a Chinese businessman wanted to talk to Chotiphatphaisal and urged him to call back to the provided number or to arrange a meeting. We ignored it, thinking that it was just another scam email.

A couple of months later, on 21 July, at approximately 11:20 hrs, one of our teammates, whose name was listed on the company board on the Department of Trade's website, informed us that a person had called him. The caller claimed to be a Chinese businessman willing to offer Sam Yan Press four million *baht* to shut down the company. They wanted to showcase dominance in Thailand to the Chinese government. They suggested that we could reopen the company afterwards. The phone number making that call and the company were the same as the earlier email. But we still believed it was a fraud and ignored it.

On 19 September the Thai agent then made an unsolicited visit to Chotiphatphaisal's family house and a temple where he had retreated as a monk. Chotiphatphaisal had not made his whereabouts public and yet they managed to find him anyway. Fortunately, Chotiphatphaisal managed to avoid meeting them. Later, on 28 September, the agency contacted us again, stating that they wanted to meet up and negotiate as soon as possible. The translated email was as follows:

I have a client, a Chinese businessman, who has tasked me with negotiating with you. The offer comprises:

"Close Nisit Sam Yan Co. Ltd. and sign a dissolution document. This involves dissolving the company, but you will still retain the ability to publish works critical of the Chinese government.

1. The cost of the dissolution process will be covered by my client.
2. The client is willing to sponsor your work and activism with 2 million *baht*.
3. The client has requested the entire process to be completed by the end of September.

Chotiphatphaisal had not made his whereabouts public, yet they managed to find him anyway

This morning, I visited Netiwit, informed him of all the details, and am now reaching out to you. Please respond or call xxxxxxxx."

Upon consulting with our lawyer, we decided to meet at the end of September, near a coffee shop in our university area. During the meeting, we inquired about the client's identity. The Thai agent claimed to have no idea about who exactly the Chinese businessman was, stating that they received the task from another Chinese agent they knew well and subsequently contacted us to deliver the offer. We rejected it, citing reasons against our ideals, and left.

We thought it was resolved and yet they called again a day later, claiming an update on the client's identity, and emailed too. The email contained a screenshot of a letter from their client, who expressed their desire for good relations with the Chinese government, clarifying they were not a party member and meant no harm. The email stated:

"In response to your concerns, I have spoken with the Chinese agency. They confirmed that:

1 If this was a security department or Chinese Communist Party operation, it would be conducted by officials, not private companies.
2 In such an operation, they would permanently close the company, the publishing house, and cease selling all books related to the Party. This is not the offer my client is making.
3 For your convenience, my client provided this confirmation letter, asserting no hostile intentions. He is not associated with the security department or the Party and pledges no harm to your reputation. He is willing to take responsibility."

We rejected the offer again. They attempted to convince us by providing another part of the letter containing a copy of the Chinese client's passport information. Again, we rejected the offer, hung up, and they finally disappeared.

While there are no known links between the Chinese businessman and

ABOVE: Netiwit Chotiphatphaisal, the founder of Sam Yan Press, is a vocal Thai student activist

China's state agencies, this incident underscores the increasing attempts to interfere with anti-China media narratives across the world. We were targets of China's attempts to silence foreign media who portrayed them in a bad light. This, however, was a peculiar incident. If the Chinese state wanted to halt our press operations, it could do so without offering a small fortune. A pertinent example is Gui Minhai, the author and bookseller, who vanished in Thailand amid rumours of working on a book about Xi Jinping's personal history. Instead, the threat came from someone who wanted to curry favour with authorities in Beijing, which shows just how far loyalties can run.

Thailand has always had a strong connection with Beijing and is a supporter of a One China policy. The Chinese Embassy in Thailand has consistently exhibited a stern and bellicose response, particularly evident in its reactions to the Milk Tea Alliance and incidents where Thais refer to Taiwan as a "country". Recently, investigations have taken place into alleged connections between "Chinese grey businesses", shady businesses that have been linked to organised crime on Thai soil and to high-profile Thai government personnel.

This incident hasn't deterred our commitment to human rights. The principle of "international solidarity" endures. Just as dictators learn from each other, so do activists. When discussing sensitive topics exposes one to government threats, supportive friends across borders can lend their voices. Sam Yan Press remained committed to its core cause. Despite financial constraints, our student-run press has vowed to continue in 2024, initiating conversations and localising the global struggle against dictatorship for Thai readers. The saga of Sam Yan Press stands as a testament to the resilience of voices against authoritarian forces and censorship. We are more determined than ever to amplify our message even in the face of daunting challenges. ✖

Jirapreeya Saeboo is managing editor of Sam Yan Press

Refused a passport

SALLY GIMSON finds out how more and more states are using passports to persecute human rights activists and dissidents abroad

HANNA KOMAR REALISED she was in trouble when she called the Belarusian embassy in London to ask whether they had her new passport. The man on the other end of the phone appeared to know exactly

SPECIAL REPORT

LEFT: Passport control at Antalya International Airport, Turkey. The country is home to many dissidents but with consulates being closed some are left with no security when they cross borders

who she was. There was no wait while he looked her name up. He just knew.

"Anna [her name in Russian]," he said. "You support sanctions with such vigour that we won't be providing you a service. Your new passport is ready and is waiting for you in Belarus. You can go and collect it there. If you have nothing to be afraid of."

Komar understood the threat. She told Index: "They were very careful not to actually deny me a passport, because they know that means I could apply for asylum or a travel document. They said only I could have one if I came to the country."

If she returns to Belarus, Komar knows she will be arrested. She has already spent nine days in prison for taking part in protests in her home country, and suffers from PTSD.

Komar is a successful poet. She is also a political activist. She has spoken and read her poems at many peaceful demonstrations in London calling for sanctions against the regime of president Alexander Lukashenko. She believes that hitting the wallets of the regime is one of the tools to help bring democratic change in Belarus. She is part of an activist group that calls itself, ironically, the People's Embassy of Belarus.

"I was very visible as an active member," she told Index. "I was absolutely reckless." At the beginning she tried wearing a mask at rallies, but after a while it seemed pointless because everyone knew who she was.

Komar did not dream that her actions would mean the embassy would essentially refuse her a new passport or identity papers. She had asked for one only because she was running out of pages for border control stamps. She is safe for now as long as her last page does not fill up too much, but in 2028 her passport will expire and she won't be able to get a new one. It will prevent her from doing lots of ordinary things: from opening a bank account in the UK to getting married.

"I fear being stateless or having no passport at all," she said, adding that she did not want to apply for asylum.

"The procedure is humiliating, it's expensive. You need a lawyer and they keep sending people back to Belarus, saying it is a safe country."

On 4 September 2023, a few weeks after Komar had spoken to the embassy, the Belarusian government announced that no Belarusian citizens living abroad would be able to get new passports at overseas embassies. This ruling affects up to half a million people who fled overseas to escape Lukashenko's regime.

Belarus is just the latest country to use the international passport system to control its citizens abroad, in what is a growing trend. Human rights activist Abdulla al-Maliki, a Qatari citizen, has spoken out about his country's abuse and exploitation of migrant workers [Index 51.3] as well as calling for democracy in Qatar and a change to what he has publicly described as a fascist, racist, terrorist and dictatorial regime. His passport ran out in 2021. He found he was not able to renew it at embassies in France and Germany and was told to return to Qatar to get a new one. He spent $50,000 on lawyers, to no avail. Al-Maliki has subsequently been tried in Qatar in absentia and sentenced to life (then on appeal to death). If he returns he will die, but without an up-to-date passport it is difficult to live abroad.

At the end of last year he was also notified by a bank official that his bank account had been frozen because of the government's refusal to renew his ID.

"I can't extend my stay in Germany and Switzerland without a passport," →

Belarus is the latest country to use the international passport system to control its citizens abroad

INDEXONCENSORSHIP.ORG **67**

→ he told Index. His only route will be to claim asylum, but he is reluctant to do that.

Amr Magdi, a senior researcher in the Middle East and North Africa division of Human Rights Watch, told Index the problem was particularly acute for people in countries where there is no recognised route to claim asylum, such as Turkey. Citizens from Turkmenistan who lived in Turkey found themselves in trouble when their government announced it would not renew their passports abroad, and encouraged them to return. According to Radio Free Europe, it is very difficult to leave Turkmenistan once back. Public sector workers have had their passports confiscated and others stopped from leaving the country at the airport despite having the right documentation. The Turkmen government has also successfully pressurised Turkey into stopping the practice of letting Turkmens work there visa-free for 30 days.

Egypt, however, is the regime with the worst track record in the world for denying passports to its citizens who live abroad. Many have fled to escape the regime of president Abdel Fattah El-Sisi. A recent report by Human Rights Watch detailed the suffering of those who have been left in limbo. Those Egyptians who ended up living in Turkey were mainly Islamists and members of the Muslim Brotherhood, according to Magdi, who did much of the research for the report. There were others, too, including Egyptians who went to Turkey for family reasons. When they tried to get passports or birth certificates, which they needed for work or to get health insurance, they found to their dismay that the Egyptian consulate in Turkey was closed. Instead, Magdi told Index, they were referred to a Facebook page. After submitting their email, they were sent a series of questions. They were asked where they lived and what they were doing as well as for links to their Facebook and Twitter accounts.

"This was really intelligence questioning, not the bureaucratic process of applying for a passport," Magdi said. "It was just a trick. The Egyptian authorities were trying to collect data about what was happening in Turkey."

It has led to people living in severe anxiety. Magdi said: "Children have been denied documents, and for children it is life-damaging. Sometimes children have lived for years without a birth certificate, with no ID. It has [even] stopped them getting vaccinations."

A few Egyptians have been able to become Turkish citizens and others have obtained leave to remain, but it is essentially at the discretion of the Turkish government.

> **They were asked where they lived and what they were doing as well as for links to their Facebook and Twitter accounts**

Many Egyptian citizens live in the Gulf. They, too, have faced difficulties. In Qatar, the embassy published lists on its Facebook page naming those who had been given appointments for new passports and those who would have to return to Egypt to get them.

There were workarounds, according to Magdi. For a while, it was possible to bribe officials in Egypt to issue passports. They would charge varying amounts according to how "complicated" the case was – namely how much was on file about them. In Jeddah, in Saudi Arabia, Egyptian diplomatic officials started issuing what turned out to be illegal paper extensions to passports. The extensions, while a useful ID for domestic purposes, left unwitting citizens open to being detained when they crossed borders for having invalid documentation.

Back in London, Komar has a specialist UK visa – a Global Talent visa – and has not stopped campaigning. She is writing a PhD on how poetry is used to share Belarusian women's experiences of domestic abuse and state violence. She is also publishing a non-fiction book describing her time in prison. But it is all overshadowed by her worries over what will happen to her when she no longer has a passport. ✖

Sally Gimson is a writer and journalist living in London

53(01):66/68|DOI:10.1177/03064220241243228

ABOVE: Belarusian activist Hanna Komar takes part in a protest in the UK. For her activism overseas she had her passport renewal effectively denied

SPECIAL REPORT

Be nice, or you're not coming in

The Indian government is revoking the status of its overseas citizens and denying visas for those critical of Modi, writes **SALIL TRIPATHI**

ABOVE: Gurpatwant Singh Pannun, a Sikh separatist leader living in the USA, was the victim of an assassination attempt in 2023. The assailant said he was acting under the orders of an Indian official

LAST JUNE, HARDEEP Singh Nijjar, a 45-year-old Sikh activist campaigning for Khalistan, a separate homeland for his co-religionists, was shot dead in British Columbia, Canada.

The murder happened in a car park, and a video emerged of his body collapsed over the steering wheel. Three months later, Canadian Prime Minister Justin Trudeau claimed there were "credible allegations" that the Indian government was involved in the murder. India reacted angrily, terming Trudeau's charge "absurd". India removed diplomats from Canada, asked Canada to reduce its diplomatic presence in India, and significantly delayed Canadian visa applications. The USA, Canada's closest ally, expressed concern but did not say more.

In recent years, India's strategic importance has increased for three reasons: its growing economy, its outwardly democratic credentials and its potential emergence as the counterweight to China – not only in Asia but on the international stage.

Western governments have been queuing up to invite Prime Minister Narendra Modi to visit their countries and rolling out the red carpet for him, or they've been visiting India and announcing investment deals – even if actual inflows may be puny compared with the bombastic claims.

Sikhs form about 2% of India's population, and most of them live in the fertile and prosperous state of Punjab along with Hindus, Muslims and others. In the early-1970s, the Shiromani Akali Dal, a political party representing Sikh and Punjabi interests, passed a resolution seeking greater autonomy. By the late 1970s, a militant movement emerged, seeking an independent homeland called Khalistan, carved out of India.

Extremists representing Khalistani interests attacked government targets and terrorised civilians. Many militants garrisoned themselves in the holiest Sikh shrine, Amritsar's Golden Temple, and in June 1984 then prime minister Indira Gandhi sent troops into the temple to eliminate the threat.

Hundreds died in what became known as Operation Bluestar. Four months later, on 31 October, Gandhi was assassinated by two of her bodyguards – both Sikh. In the retaliatory violence that followed, thousands of Sikhs were killed in northern India.

Indian security forces pursued the militants ruthlessly, and the Khalistan movement subsided. It survives among Sikhs abroad who dream of an independent Sikh nation, but in India there is little support for Sikh separatism. →

> When I sought out some of the academics denied entry, none of them wanted to speak – on or off the record

→ However, Sikhs overseas and in India remember the attack on the Golden Temple, the pogrom of Sikhs in 1984 and the lack of justice. While Indian leaders have since expressed regret over the violence, and a Sikh economist – Manmohan Singh – was India's prime minister from 2004 until 2014, the wounds have not healed. That accounts for the nostalgic longing for an independent homeland among some Sikhs abroad.

Nijjar's killing would have remained largely forgotten, but in November the USA charged an Indian national, Nikhil Gupta, with attempting to hire an assassin to kill Gurpatwant Singh Pannun, a Sikh separatist leader who is the general counsel for Sikhs for Justice and who lives in the USA. Gupta, the USA alleged, was acting under the directions of an Indian government official and had offered $100,000 to a potential assassin.

He did not know that the man he was trying to hire was, in fact, a US agent, and Gupta is now in a Czech jail, awaiting extradition to the USA.

While the Indian government denied any role, its response to the US charge was more muted and less full of bluster than its response to Trudeau. US President Joe Biden was invited as the guest of honour to India's day of pomp and glory – the Republic Day parade – in January this year. Biden did not make the trip and while he did not give any specific reason, diplomatic circles believe it was meant as a snub to India, which has elections later this year. The incumbent Modi would have loved the footage of Biden by his side, watching the might of India's defence forces marching by.

There is no evidence of India's role in either Nijjar's murder or the plot against Pannun, and they could just as easily have been rogue operations. But the US charge-sheet is fairly detailed, and India's subdued response raises questions. India's current government has long admired the long reach of →

PICTURED: A meeting between Canadian Prime Minister Justin Trudeau and Indian Prime Minister Narendra Modi in 2018, before tensions escalated between the two over the killing of a Sikh separatist leader in suburban Vancouver

The US charge-sheet is fairly detailed, and India's subdued response raises questions

→ Israel's Mossad, which has a record of carrying out spectacular attacks against those Israel considers its enemies.

Could some Indian officials have been tempted to imitate Israel as a form of flattery?

Carrying out violent acts against individuals or organisations that a government considers hostile to its interests in a friendly country is an extreme form of transnational repression. But India has practised many other subtler forms of preventing contact between Indian dissidents seeking a global platform and foreign researchers or journalists wishing to report on India. It has expelled journalists, prevented academics from entering the country, stopped its own journalists or human rights activists from travel and got Indian embassies to complain loudly against foreign reporting of India.

Most recently, Vanessa Dougnac, who had been the longest-staying foreign correspondent in India, said she would leave the country after India revoked her status as an Overseas Citizen of India (OCI). (She is married to an Indian national, and so qualifies for such a status.) The title is misleading: OCI does not grant any citizenship rights such as the right to vote, but it grants the individual a permanent, long-stay visa and the ability to work (except in certain sectors). Dougnac was told her reporting for various French publications created a "biased, negative" perception of India. She wrote a heartfelt lament while leaving the country she considers her own, saying the government's onerous conditions made it impossible for her to work there.

Earlier, the overseas citizenship of Ashok Swain, who teaches peace and conflict studies at Uppsala University in Sweden, was revoked. In November 2020, Swain was informed his OCI would be revoked because of his "inflammatory speeches" and "anti-India activities". Swain asked for specific instances and requested for the decision to be overturned so he could visit his unwell mother back in India. His request was denied.

Swain sued the government, and in July 2023 the court ruled in his favour, saying the government needed to provide proper reasons. Later that month, the Indian embassy in Stockholm sent him another note, long on rhetoric and short on specifics, saying he was "hurting religious sentiments", "destabilising" India's social fabric and "spreading hate propaganda". Swain was tweeting too much and too critically about India, the order said, hurting the country's image abroad. Swain's case will be heard in May.

The OCI status was created not as a right but as a privilege or an entitlement, because people of Indian origin who lived abroad had been clamouring for dual nationality, which Indian laws don't permit. It was created in 2005 under the 1955 Citizenship Act, which allows foreign citizens of Indian origin or foreigners married to Indian citizens to enter the country without a visa and reside, work and hold property there, among other benefits.

But lately the government is wary of OCI journalists and academics visiting or living in the country, especially if the government does not like their reporting or investigations. In March 2021, India required OCIs to seek a permit to conduct research, for mountaineering, for missionary, journalistic or Tablighi (a Muslim sect) activities, or to visit any area of India deemed as "protected".

According to the human rights and law-focused web portal Article 14, which has examined the issue in great detail, more than 4.5 million people around the world are OCIs, and data released by the government in response to an inquiry under India's Right to Information Act, showed that the Modi administration had cancelled at least 102 OCI cards between 2014 and May 2023. In theory, those whose OCIs are cancelled can apply for a regular visa to visit India, but the government reserves the right to blacklist them which would, in effect, bar them forever from entering the country.

In November 2022, 82-year-old UK-based activist Amrit Wilson received a letter that tore to shreds her official ties with India. The letter, from the Indian high commission, blamed her for "anti-India activities" and for making "detrimental propaganda" which was "inimical" to India's sovereignty and integrity. There was, of course, no evidence – but she was asked to provide reasons within a fortnight why her status should not be revoked. Wilson sent a detailed response, but several months later the government replied that her response wasn't "plausible", and cancelled her status. She is now appealing through the Indian court system. In its response, the government pointed out some of her tweets for being critical of the government and an article that opposed the revoking of the special status granted to the erstwhile state of Jammu and Kashmir.

The government claims it can cancel the status of those who have shown "disaffection to the constitution" or "assisted an enemy during war", or done anything that it believes is against the interests of "sovereignty, integrity and security" of India.

Chetan Ahimsa (Kumar), a leading actor in Kannada films, had his status revoked briefly, too. Ahimsa is a US citizen. He was arrested in India after he criticised a ban on Muslim students wearing the hijab in schools in the southern state of Karnataka. In court, the government said India could expel people who were "undesirable" and foreigners did not have the right to free speech in India. The court stayed the cancellation.

More famously, in 2019, the USA-based writer Aatish Taseer, whose mother is the Indian journalist Tavleen Singh and whose father is the slain Pakistani politician Salman Taseer, had his overseas citizenship cancelled after he wrote a cover story in Time magazine asking if India could survive another five years of Modi. In Taseer's case, the government claimed his status was revoked because he had "concealed" the fact that his father was a Pakistani national. Earlier, in 2014, Christine Mehta, a researcher at Amnesty International, had her OCI revoked after she studied India's human rights record in Jammu and Kashmir.

A web-based portal called Disinfo Lab has, according to a report in The Washington Post, been compiling information of critics overseas, Indian or not, and blaming them for undermining India. The portal establishes links between the critics and the philanthropic billionaire George Soros, sometimes by connecting disconnected dots, to present an image of a gigantic conspiracy.

At the same time, foreign-based web portals critical of India are being taken offline inside the country. The latest to suffer such erasure is Hindutva Watch, which compiled human rights violations by Hindu fundamentalists. India has escalated demands on X, formerly Twitter, and many accounts critical of the government have been "withheld" recently, including those operated by foreigners who live abroad. X has complied, but issued a statement expressing disapproval of the government's action. Clearly, X's owner Elon Musk, who claims to champion free speech, has a different standard for different countries, and in the Indian case, he has meekly complied with many requests.

Academics are also being turned away. Within weeks of Modi's election in 2014, Penny Vera-Sanso, of Birkbeck University in London, who had been visiting India since 1990 and writes about gender, was denied entry. In 2022, Lindsay Bremner, who teaches architecture at the University of Westminster, had a valid research visa when she arrived in India, but was told at the airport that she could not enter. Earlier that year, Flippo Osella, who teaches anthropology at the University of Sussex, was sent back. He is an expert on Kerala and has been visiting India for 30 years. The government claimed his research on caste was deemed "sensitive". Osella understands Malayalam and has studied the Ezhava community. He has written about Mamootty, a popular actor in Kerala, and was working with local institutions on predicting weather. His research was supported by the UK government, but he was treated brusquely and not allowed to contact friends in India.

India has also barred writers and academics who have tourist visas but who might conduct research, which would technically violate Indian rules. In 2018, Kathryn Hummel, an Australian poet, was turned away at Bangalore airport and Pakistani researcher Annie Zaman was similarly sent back and prevented from attending a conference in Delhi. When I sought out some of the academics denied entry, none of them wanted to speak, on or off the record, because they did not wish to jeopardise their visas in the future. Some American journalists, Indian origin or otherwise, too have had visa requests delayed or denied.

When graduate students and academics at several US universities organised a three-day conference in 2021 called Dismantling Global Hindutva, which examined the rise of Hindu nationalism in India and its effects on Indian society, several academics and potential speakers were warned off from participating, and a few backed out, so as not to jeopardise future visits to India. Indian residents in the USA who support the Indian government wrote to faculty heads and university administrators complaining against those academics. Academics in the USA who are of Indian origin and are critical of India have frequently been targeted by concerted efforts from pro-government overseas Indians, calling for their dismissal or for them to be disciplined.

Several journalists and human rights activists living in India find themselves mired in legal cases, which means they must have clearance from courts or other appropriate authorities before leaving the country. This has prevented several writers and human rights activists from participating at events overseas.

Others with clean records also find that they are suspect. Sanna Irshad Mattoo, a Kashmiri photojournalist whose photographs earned her the Pulitzer Prize in 2022, was prevented from leaving for Paris to launch a book featuring her work, even though she had a valid French visa.

India is erecting a barrier between scholars and their subjects, reporters and their stories, and closing off doors and windows, narrowing Indian minds and hardening outlooks.

And it flexes its muscles abroad, shouting at critics, preventing their travel and access, and – if the Canadian and US accusations are true – attempting to eliminate those it disagrees with.

But it will hold elections in a few months, and encomiums praising the world's largest democracy will follow. Naturally. ✘

Salil Tripathi is Index's South Asia contributing editor

He was treated brusquely and not allowed to contact friends in India

An agency for those denied agency

A press agency is giving a voice to Sikhs who are coming under attack globally, writes **AMY FALLON**

ABOVE: An image from India's farmers' protests, which Sikh PA covered

"IF IT WEREN'T for the Sikh Press Association, a lot of Sikh voices, especially ours, wouldn't be heard," Deepa Singh told Index, just months after he said he was treated like a terrorist in the UK.

His is one of those who has benefited from a press agency giving a voice to those who may not otherwise have one.

The founder of the charity Sikh Youth UK, who is also known as Kaldip Singh Lehal, was arrested at Gatwick Airport while returning to the UK last December. He said he was subjected to a humiliating detainment and "interrogation…like a terrorist" under the government's counter-terror law – and he told his story to the Sikh PA.

This agency provides multi-platform content – including editorial copy, news, images, infographics, video content and data – to journalists and newsrooms around the world. The idea emerged in 2012, during a massive explosion of online Sikh education, when one man had a vision. The late Bhai Jagraj Singh was an Oxford graduate and a former British Army officer who gave up a successful career in finance to found the Sikh PA in London.

A news agency for the world's fifth largest faith group, and run by a team of just two, is a big deal. It provided coverage of the 2020 and 2021 farmers' protests against laws passed by the Indian parliament. It also reported on the assassination of Sikh activist Hardeep Singh Nijjar in Canada in June 2023. Canada has accused India of carrying this out, an accusation it denies.

But "censorship and targeted interference remain barriers" to the agency's work, said Everything's 13, the Sikh educational charity under which Sikh PA operates. Its press officers have received threatening phone calls after covering certain issues, while online death threats are a frequent occurrence, Jasveer Singh, the press executive at Sikh PA, told Index.

Originally from the UK, he now works for the agency in British Columbia, Canada, which has a large Sikh population.

"There have also been character attacks which involve tarnishing the reputation of staff, legal threats and even efforts to have the association labelled an extremist organisation," he said.

He added that while some of those behind these attacks may be "Indian nationalist bots" and not real people, "if they're willing to threaten someone like me, then the people that are active who are bringing thousands together to be part of this movement…they want them killed".

A former staff member was prevented from entering India because of his journalism, he said.

Because the West "became apathetic to Indian interference, overlooking it for trade deals", borders do not keep the community safe, he said. Support for Khalistan (a separatist movement promoting the idea of a Sikh homeland) and criticism of India have increased, while India has stepped up its efforts to silence activists.

Meanwhile, Jasveer claims enclaves have appeared in the diaspora where violent criminal Indian nationalist gangs work.

"But Sikh faith is entwined with tales of courage and sacrifice," he said, adding that carrying out the work of Bhai Jagraj Singh, who died in 2017 aged just 38, is a "task of honour".

"We are the voice for the voiceless, a megaphone for the unheard of our community," he said. "That must continue regardless." ✖

Amy Fallon is an Australian-Canadian journalist

> If they're willing to threaten someone like me, then the people that are active who are bringing thousands together to be part of this movement…they want them killed

Always looking behind

China is one of the main perpetrators of transnational repression worldwide. Just how long has Beijing been at it? How have they changed the rules of the game? Index invited two prominent Chinese dissidents to talk about their own personal experiences of moving to the other side of the world to protect themselves from persecution by the Chinese state only to find themselves stilll in danger, looking over their shoulder.

Tiananmen protest leader **ZHOU FENGSUO** writes about navigating decades of threats in the USA, some of which now also come from a more nationalistic Chinese diaspora.

NATHAN LAW, one of the faces of Hong Kong's democracy movement, talks about now having a bounty on his head and never walking the same route home.

Both are high-profile and not afforded anonymity, something which means they are doubly exposed through being so recognised. But their fame can shield them to an extent too. Other overseas targets of Beijing who are less well-known can be just as ruthlessly pursued without an international community having their back. Ultimately their stories, which overlap, speak of just what dissidents suffer and often suffer silently.

ABOVE: Zhou Fengsuo unveils a bust of Chinese Nobel Peace Prize winner Liu Xiaobo, who died after long imprisonment in China, in Prague, Czech Republic, 2019

Zhou Fengsuo

I was a student leader in Tiananmen because I wanted to do my duty for the country. I was proud of what I did, knowing that I had done so much to help facilitate the movement for a peaceful transition of China into a freer and more democratic China. But for this I was put on the most wanted list after the massacre. I was in position number five. From then on my life took on a different tune. I was arrested and put in a high-security jail in Beijing for a year and had my passport denied for five years. As soon as I got it I left China for the USA. It was January 1995.

The transition to the USA was not problem free, even from the start. I went to business school and got an MBA with honours and became a financial professional. Initially I was very relaxed but soon I realised I was very isolated from the ordinary Chinese community here. It seemed I bore a mark on my head wherever I went. People didn't want to get close to me. Worse still, employers avoided me. Most of my friends at business school who were from China got jobs easily, but I couldn't, even though my grades were really good. Wall Street banks were very concerned about the political risks of socialising with people like me. I was →

> Wang, who has been serving life in prison in China since 2002, must have been monitored

→ told by a Human Resources manager that the most high-profile female leader from 1989 Chai Ling was denied a job opportunity in New York because the Chairman of the Asian branch of the investment bank that offered her a job objected vehemently.

There was one incident that happened when I was in business school that also really alarmed me. In the spring of 1998 I met Wang Bingzhang, the most famous Chinese dissident. A few months later my family called and mentioned this meeting. They knew about it and what we'd talked about. Wang, who has been serving life in prison in China since 2002, must have been monitored. So it was a warning to me. The MSS [China's Ministry of State Security] was telling me that even though I was in the USA they could still keep a close eye.

Still, I was largely oblivious to safety concerns in the early days and I continued my activism, including cofounding my own humanitarian organisation to support political prisoners in China.

The worst moment for me was in 2008. That year, when the Beijing Olympics happened, was the peak of China business. In San Francisco when the Olympic torch was passing by, we were beaten very brutally by CCP supporters. It was probably the largest gathering of CCP supporters on US soil ever – there were over 100,000 supporters, compared to just a handful of us protesters – and they really attacked us physically. I asked police to protect us, but they just shrugged and watched. This was the worst moment. I was surrounded by so many angry, impassioned CCP supporters. I believe they were ready to kill us. Their hatred of people like us was visceral. My friend Guo Ping was bleeding from an attack on the back of his head that could have been fatal.

Later I called all the major papers and TV stations in the United States about it but nobody responded.

Since Xi Jinping came to power it has become way more aggressive both on the ground and online. Even though I didn't experience anything like what happened in 2008 again, I have known many attacks here, especially the attacks on the Hong Kong community in 2019. They were very extensive and well-organised. I wasn't at the protests in San Francisco last November when Xi visited for the APEC summit. Once again protesters were attacked by CCP followers. Once again we published a report on it because we knew it wouldn't otherwise be covered.

In 2018, after I organised a protest against Xi as leader for life, someone came to my house and used a big camera to take pictures, knowing I was inside. I realised this was a warning and also they are not trying to hide at all. It's much more brazen and well-organised. Xi Jinping's message is to go strong and to go after critics aboard.

They have become very sophisticated in how they threaten us. They gather all information on us that they can from publicly available sources. We know our organisation has everything closely examined by CCP. They scooped up all my personal information online too and organised a massive slandering and intimidation campaign against me on social media. My organisation's public filings were used to harass us and to disrupt our work.

I even heard from a good source who was told the CCP would use US law and the US legal system to go after them. In FBI reported cases of the CCP spying on dissidents, tax records are often sought as a way to intimidate and coerce people and organisations.

Since 2020 US law enforcement has started to take action against those perpetrators of transnational repression and Congress is more aware too. But overall the CCP's influence remains strong and pervasive in all areas of life. We will not be daunted. We will fight to be free, not to be silenced by fear.

Nathan Law

In June 2020, I made the difficult decision to leave Hong Kong. As a former protest leader and legislator, my outspoken criticism of Beijing had effectively painted a target on my back. The ramification of being a high-profile dissident became clear in August when the Hong Kong police, enforcing the draconian national security law newly imposed, issued arrest warrants for six democracy activists living abroad, myself included. The situation escalated in July 2023, when a bounty of 1 million Hong Kong dollars was placed on me, underscoring the lengths to which Beijing is willing to go to silence its critics beyond its borders. This pursuit is a testament to the concept of transnational repression, where authoritarian regimes extend their reach across the globe to target dissidents.

I was granted asylum in the United Kingdom in April 2021, but the threats from the Chinese Communist Party loomed large. I moved four times in the first year, living a discrete life, and had to be aware of my surroundings constantly to avoid tailing. The extended reach of the CCP was further highlighted when a UK-based anonymous group of Chinese overseas offered a reward for information about my whereabouts. I was not sure whether anyone offered them any intelligence – but the fact that they are so blatantly threatening exiled activists shows the CCP's arrogance and aggression. As a result, I was always in doubt when connecting with

ABOVE: Nathan Law attends a candle-lit vigil organised outside the Chinese Embassy in London in memory of those who died in the 1989 Tiananmen Massacre

new individuals because they could approach me with ulterior motives.

The repercussions of my activism were not limited to just myself. To frighten me, my family was subjected to interrogation by the Hong Kong police under false pretences of supporting my work financially. This baseless harassment aimed to inflict guilt and fear, leveraging collateral damage to the well-being of my loved ones. They were extremely bothered and scared. Friends in Hong Kong who were close to them told me this in secret.

The threats extend into the digital realm, where Beijing's vast online propaganda machine orchestrates campaigns of vilification against its critics. Death threats and doxxing are part of the harassment I face, a constant reminder of the risks that come with dissent.

Escaping the grasp of an authoritarian regime is just the beginning of an ongoing struggle for freedom. The incidents of transnational repression are a reminder that the fight against autocracy doesn't end at the border. It's imperative for host countries of political refugees to recognise the sophisticated tactics of authoritarian regimes and ensure the safety of exiled activists. Their continued activism is vital, not just for their home countries, but as a beacon for democratic values worldwide. ✖

Zhou Fengsuo was a leader of the Tiananmen Square protest movement. He lives in the USA

Nathan Law is a political exile based in the UK. He was one of the main organisers of various protest movements in Hong Kong

> The fact that they are so blatantly threatening exiled activists shows the CCP's arrogance and aggression

Putting Interpol on notice

Calls are growing for a revamp of the Red Notice system, amid evidence that the current set-up is playing into authoritarian hands, writes **TOMMY GREENE**

INTERNATIONAL CONCERN IS growing around the abuse of Interpol Red Notices, as victims and human rights groups call for deterrent-based reforms to the alerts system.

Tens of thousands of Red Notices – requests to "law enforcement worldwide to locate and provisionally arrest a person pending extradition, surrender or similar legal action", usually following a court order or arrest warrant in the applicant country – are issued by the international policing organisation every year. The organisation's data indicates that fewer than 5% of them are cancelled or deleted each year.

With little published data on the system's operations amid a volatile geopolitical climate, human rights groups warn that the international crime agency alerts are increasingly being abused by authoritarian governments, with a number of countries emerging as notorious repeat offenders.

"The first thing with the Red Notice system is it's very attractive to dictatorial regimes," said Rhys Davies, a UK-based human rights barrister. It allows such actors to extend policing reach "well beyond their own borders" and "use other countries' open society mechanisms" to harass and intimidate critics.

"If you're on this list, you're likely going to get arrested," he said. "Lots of countries, even developed jurisdictions, will treat these as de facto arrest warrants – which they're not. They take the requests, in general terms, at face value. So when there is a degree of scrutiny, it's after the event."

A number of high-profile cases involving the apparent harassment of journalists and activists – sometimes for "nakedly political" ends, Davies said – have recently thrown the system's alleged misuse into sharp relief.

> International crime agency alerts are increasingly being abused by authoritarian governments

LEFT: Interpol officers in Colombia ahead of an operation extraditing a drug lord in 2022, a known criminal as opposed to a dissident

> It is used by China deliberately to evade the legal protections built into legitimate systems of extradition

British journalist Clare Rewcastle Brown was forced to flee Spain earlier this year after news of a surprise defamation conviction emerged from Malaysia, which she described as "political revenge" for her public-interest reporting in the country. (She said Spain has a poorer record than the UK on arrests once Red Notices are issued, so she went back to the UK once she found out about the ruling in absentia.)

Malaysia had previously unsuccessfully applied for two Red Notices on charges relating to her explosive investigation into the multi-billion dollar 1MDB scandal, which implicated the country's jailed former prime minister, Najib Razak. It is unclear whether the Malaysian authorities have now applied for a third Red Notice but, Rewcastle Brown told Index, just knowing they may have done so has a "chilling effect" and stops her from doing her journalistic work in the region where she had been based.

"The other problem I was warned of, which I have to be wary of, is that it's not just Interpol – Malaysia has all sorts of bilateral policing arrangements and it raises questions wherever I travel, particularly in South-East Asia," she said.

"So you can be on people's systems all over the world – you just don't know when or where you're going to be pulled up."

She added that the British government had "not volunteered to do anything to protect its citizen in this matter", forcing her to rely on support from NGOs.

More than a dozen of them – including Index – sent a joint complaint to Interpol over the first Red Notice application for Rewcastle Brown. This prompted the organisation's chief, Jürgen Stock, to issue a statement declaring that it would be rejected – an unusual step in such cases.

Another recent high-profile case saw Uyghur activist Idris Hasan facing extradition from Morocco to China after a Red Notice was issued in March 2021. Despite an international outcry and the Red Notice having been annulled in August the same year, Hasan remains in detention in Morocco.

"It has particular value for China as many nations don't have extradition treaties with Beijing," Ted Bromund, a senior research fellow at the Heritage Foundation think tank, said of the Red Notice system during an event at the UK's parliament last year. "And it is used by China deliberately to evade the legal protections built into legitimate systems of extradition."

Fighting such alerts and associated extradition requests is invariably resource-intensive. Financier and high-profile Kremlin critic Bill Browder was able to drum up international support – tweeting then-UK foreign secretary Boris Johnson, among others – to help him fight one of seven Red Notices that Russia had applied for in relation to his campaigning activities.

Successfully resisting prolonged detention and extradition requests made under these alerts can come down to a geopolitical lottery, Davies said, alongside "having to have the wherewithal to instruct lawyers, to be able to know the system or to know you can do this".

He added: "And you also need to keep your fingers crossed that you haven't been arrested in, say, a country that's friendly to China – of which there are many nowadays."

Since many Red Notices are scrutinised only "on the way out rather than on the way in", he added, "quite often it's too late" for those fighting extradition and seeking liberty.

An increasing number of people appear to be slipping through the net. Bahraini dissident Ahmed Jaafar Mohamed Ali was extradited to the Gulf state before being imprisoned and tortured. He was given two life sentences after his 2021 arrest in Serbia under a Red Notice alert. He is now suing Interpol over the "unlawful" processes.

Some say Interpol is in denial about questions of reform. Stock, however, argues it has come a long way on curbing abusive Red Notice applications and is doing all it can to root them out.

"We have a small percentage, maybe 2%, 3%, of tricky notices," he told Reuters last year. "The overwhelming majority concern murderers, rapists, drug smugglers and what have you."

Stock added that more checks had been introduced earlier in the process, with all requests now being screened before Red Notices are issued. He said Interpol could not do much more for now to improve the system.

"Because of the increasing number of Red Notices," Davies said, "instances of miscarriages of justice are increasing."

Victims of abusive Red Notices have suggested a number of deterrents to discourage such activity.

"Firstly, Interpol has to be prepared to name and shame people who play the system and/or act in bad faith," Davies said. "Secondly, there needs to be a wider degree of scrutiny in terms of what information goes in. And then, finally, you need to have the democratic nations who pay the bills for Interpol demanding some sort of reform." ✖

Tommy Greene is a journalist, writer and translator

Living in Russia's shadow

The death of Putin's greatest opponent Alexei Navalny this year has shaken the Kremlin's critics. After being poisoned on his way to Siberia and receiving treatment in Germany, he made the fateful decision to return to Russia, where he was thrown behind bars. What happened to him was tragic, and perhaps predictable. But leaving Russia behind isn't always enough to keep dissidents safe. Over the years, some of the most brazen cases of repression across borders have included the tragic poisoning of Alexander Litvinenko in London in 2006 and the attempted assassination of Sergei and Yulia Skripal in Salisbury in 2018. There are many more suspected cases: plane crashes, supposed suicides and mysterious neck fractures. For Russians speaking out, the stakes really are high. How then, do the Kremlin's critics navigate their daily lives, when something as simple as a cup of tea can pose a threat?

Three Russian journalists have shared their experiences with Index. Echo of Moscow radio host **IRINA BABLOYAN** is living with the after effects of a suspected poisoning in Georgia, and has had to change how she goes about everyday life to keep herself safe. Author of The Compatriots, **ANDREI SOLDATOV**, unravels the bureaucratic measures he faces, the lawsuit that threatens to silence him and the possible penalty should he take a misstep abroad. And for editor-in-chief of Novaya Gazeta, **KIRILL MARTYNOV**, being declared a "foreign agent" leaves him at risk of prosecution in absentia.

A life after poisoning

Borders have not kept Echo of Moscow radio host **IRINA BABLOYAN** safe. A suspected poisoning changed her life, and she is now on a heightened state of alert

BOTTLES, TABLETS, TUBES of hormonal creams – instead of the usual things you'd find in a woman's cosmetics bag, these items are always with me now. There's no logic in when my symptoms will appear, and doctors still haven't made a diagnosis. I can be on air in the middle of my radio show, which is quite a nerve-wracking job, wandering on holiday in a new city, or just sleeping, and suddenly my body starts to break out in red spots, sometimes burns.

Sometimes it's in only one area, and sometimes I'm covered from head to toe by an allergic reaction. Opening a bottle of water, turning on the tap in the bathroom, opening the front door with a key or simply pulling the door handle – for me, any of these actions can mean doing nothing else with my hands

SPECIAL REPORT

ABOVE: Alexei Navalny speaks at the Echo of Moscow radio station, where Irina Babloyan now works

for the next 10 minutes, and sometimes longer. My hands instantly go numb and it's very painful to move my fingers. It is suspected that this is all a result of a poisoning in Tbilisi in October 2022, but the results of my tests at Charité hospital in Berlin were lost.

Two years ago, I was naïve enough to think that leaving Russia would immediately make us safe. In Russia, if you're an independent journalist, you're always on alert. You understand that the special services may be waiting for you at home for a conversation, as has happened to me more than once. They may come to search, beat you, break your fingers while telling you not to write anymore – and even kill you. You live with an understanding of this.

When many of us left Russia, it seemed like we were safe. The sense of alarm diminished a bit – but it turned out to be in vain.

After what happened to me and Novaya Gazeta journalist Elena Kostyuchenko (a suspected poisoning in Germany, also in October 2022), a detective from the Berlin police (I now live in Germany) called me in for questioning.

During the interrogation, he asked me: "Do you feel safe here?" I couldn't even answer that question right away. I didn't want to seem paranoid.

Then he asked me: "Do you consider it safe for you to be in Germany?"

I replied "No", knowing that my other colleagues in exile could also be in danger. It sounds wild and it's often very difficult to explain to people from non-autocratic countries that we are persecuted for our work.

Now, when I need to go somewhere, I try not to write about it anywhere and tell only people close to me. Posting my location on social media is out of the question. I don't allow others to film me, and if a friend takes a photo, I ask them to post it later – at least a day or two later.

Buying a plane ticket has become much more expensive because I usually do it either on the day or a day before the trip. In hotels, I drink only from new, sealed bottles. At parties, I don't let go of my glass. If I leave it for a moment, I go for a new drink and closely watch the bartenders.

I almost always refuse public appearances and often ignore events where crowds of Russian journalists and activists are gathered. Sometimes there's no opportunity to skip the event, and then I'm very careful about my behaviour and the people around me.

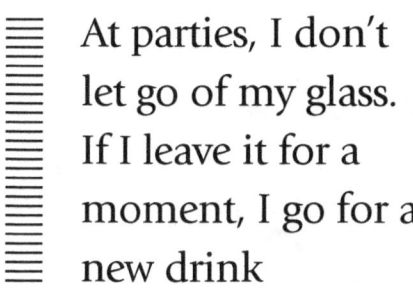

At parties, I don't let go of my glass. If I leave it for a moment, I go for a new drink

If I have suspicions about a particular person, I ask the organisers and security.

Eating at restaurants is very difficult. I know some colleagues who no longer eat in public places at all, and some even go out with security. But these are just the basic measures that are not so difficult to follow. There are a number of other things that I cannot tell you for safety reasons.

But life goes on. I've already adapted to all the new rules and continue to work. Work keeps me sane.

Irina Babloyan is a Russian journalist with radio station Echo of Moscow, who lives in Berlin

Rinse and repeat

Russia is learning lessons from its silencing successes, only adding to the list of threats to journalists, writes ANDREI SOLDATOV

IN JANUARY, THE Russian State Duma introduced a bill which would allow the confiscation of property from those convicted of crimes against the state, including "spreading deliberately false information" about the war in Ukraine. The main targets are Russian journalists, most of them in exile.

Many of my colleagues and I needed to make a mental check on any property, cars or bank accounts that could be targeted.

Since the start of the invasion, the Kremlin has been inventive in trying →

ABOVE: The aftermath of the attempted assassination of Russian spy Sergei Skripal and his daughter, who were victims of a nerve agent attack in Salisbury, UK

→ to silence our voices. This is why most of us found ourselves to be the targets of an impressive collection of measures applied by the authorities.

In my case, the website Agentura.ru is blocked in Russia. My words cannot be cited in the country's media without the description of "foreign agent"; I don't travel to certain countries which could extradite me to Russia, where I face up to 10 years in jail because I'm on the wanted list (for spreading "fake news about the war"); and my accounts in Russian banks have been blocked since 2022.

There are also bureaucratic measures which seem small on the surface but which could make lives of journalists in exile much harder. For instance, the recently introduced legislation lets Russian consulates confiscate our passports. Most of us still live, and travel, on our Russian passports. When they expire, we need to renew them but since December this option is no longer available to us.

And yet the journalists remain active, and this clearly infuriates the Kremlin.

The new battlefields are the German courts.

In October 2023, Russian businessman Alexei Kozlov went to the Hamburg district court and secured a ban on German sales of audio and e-book copies of The Compatriots, a book I published with my co-author Irina Borogan in 2019. The book tells the story of the difficult relationship between Russian émigrés and the Kremlin's intelligence agencies.

Kozlov, who lives in Berlin but travels regularly to Moscow, began his action in September, four years after publication of the book. Kozlov disagreed "that he made his professional career with the support [of] and due to personal connections" in the KGB. Kozlov is a scion of a prominent family of Soviet spies – his great-grandfather was Stalin's undercover intelligence chief in the USA while his step-great-grandfather organised Trotsky's murder on Stalin's orders.

Kozlov decided to sue our publisher, Hachette, to attack our credibility. He said on Facebook: "It will be difficult for them to pass a reputation audit from normal media. For them, as for 'experts', this will be a black spot for their entire life."

It appears some lessons were learned from the long and costly legal battle of 2021 over Putin's People, a book by the Financial Times's former Moscow correspondent Catherine Belton. Several Russian oligarchs sued Belton's publisher, HarperCollins.

Several journalists told us afterwards that it had become more difficult after the case for authors to get a book about

Russia accepted by a publisher.

It's unlikely the Kremlin will have missed the lesson.

These days, Russian journalists in exile always keep in mind that our devices could be compromised; we are extra careful which countries we visit; we remain concerned about the pressure that could be put on our relatives in Russia; and we are aware of the legal risks we face in our host countries.

It is a heavy package – and one which is unlikely to get lighter.

Andrei Soldatov is a Russian investigative journalist and author

A foreigner in my own land

The threats faced by journalists in exile serve as a warning to those still in Russia, writes KIRILL MARTYNOV

SINCE THE BEGINNING of the full-scale war against Ukraine, hundreds of thousands of people have left Russia, including a significant number of political activists and journalists. We faced a choice: to end up in prison at home for our anti-war statements or to continue our work abroad.

While Russia now has hundreds of new political prisoners (and we share a deep grief because of Alexei Navalny's murder in a prison beyond the Arctic Circle), a large number of supporters of democratic Russia chose exile. Russian authorities regularly create new threats for their opponents who find themselves abroad. I believe these transboundary repressions against emigrants are primarily needed to intimidate Russians who remain in the country. If people see that there is an alternative to dictatorship and war, Vladimir Putin's regime will face a severe crisis.

At the heart of the transboundary censorship organised by the Kremlin is the law on foreign agents. Actually, most of the independent public figures in Russia are already labelled foreign agents by the Kremlin.

I personally have been declared a foreign agent in Russia, which means that criminal proceedings can be initiated against me at any time. I am not personally offended, considering that current Putin-era laws allow for the persecution of such individuals under multiple criminal articles.

These are individuals who oppose war, who establish non-profit organisations abroad after the ban of our media in Russia, who interact with foreigners, who write about the crimes of the Russian army in Ukraine and who support the LGBTQ+ community.

The foreign agent law means that I have no access to bank accounts in Russia, and if I had any property remaining there it could be seized. Relatives of foreign agents face persecution and pressure from the police, and we anticipate more such cases this year.

As journalists, we work for a Russian audience, but the restrictions imposed on foreign agents prohibit me from entering into advertising contracts with Russian companies. For example, I cannot give lectures at Russian universities, even remotely. The foreign agent law essentially imposes a ban on any public activity for the Russian audience, even if you are abroad. This law is specifically enacted to destroy the most popular Russian bloggers and journalists working from abroad.

Formally, it requires marking any of your statements with a special text indicating the "agent" status, and also regularly reporting to the government on all personal income and expenses.

Many lawyers and notaries refuse to represent our interests in the country, and the books of foreign agents are prohibited from being published. We also have several cases of criminal prosecution because of violating foreign agent rules, so people abroad can be put on the international list of wanted criminals by the Russian government.

The next level of transboundary censorship is the label "undesirable organisation". In addition to being personally designated a foreign agent, I also lead two undesirable organisations – the newspaper Novaya Gazeta Europe and Free Moscow University. Any contact with them by Russians can lead to criminal cases, as these laws also have extra-territorial effects. The state regards us as its property, and there is a practice of prosecuting emigrants in absentia and in absentia-arrests.

This status means Russians are prohibited from co-operating with "undesirable" foreign organisations regardless of their location. In the case of media, this poses a threat not only to journalists working from Russia but also to our sources and heroes. We are forced to conceal their names or publish our stories with partners to protect people from persecution and involvement with an "undesirable organisation".

And, of course, if the status of a foreign agent and an undesirable organisation is not enough to silence you, there is always the list of "terrorists and extremists"…

Kirill Martynov is editor-in-chief of independent media outlet Novaya Gazeta Europe, and labelled as a foreign agent by Russian authorities ✖

> If people see that there is an alternative to dictatorship and war, Putin's regime will face a severe crisis

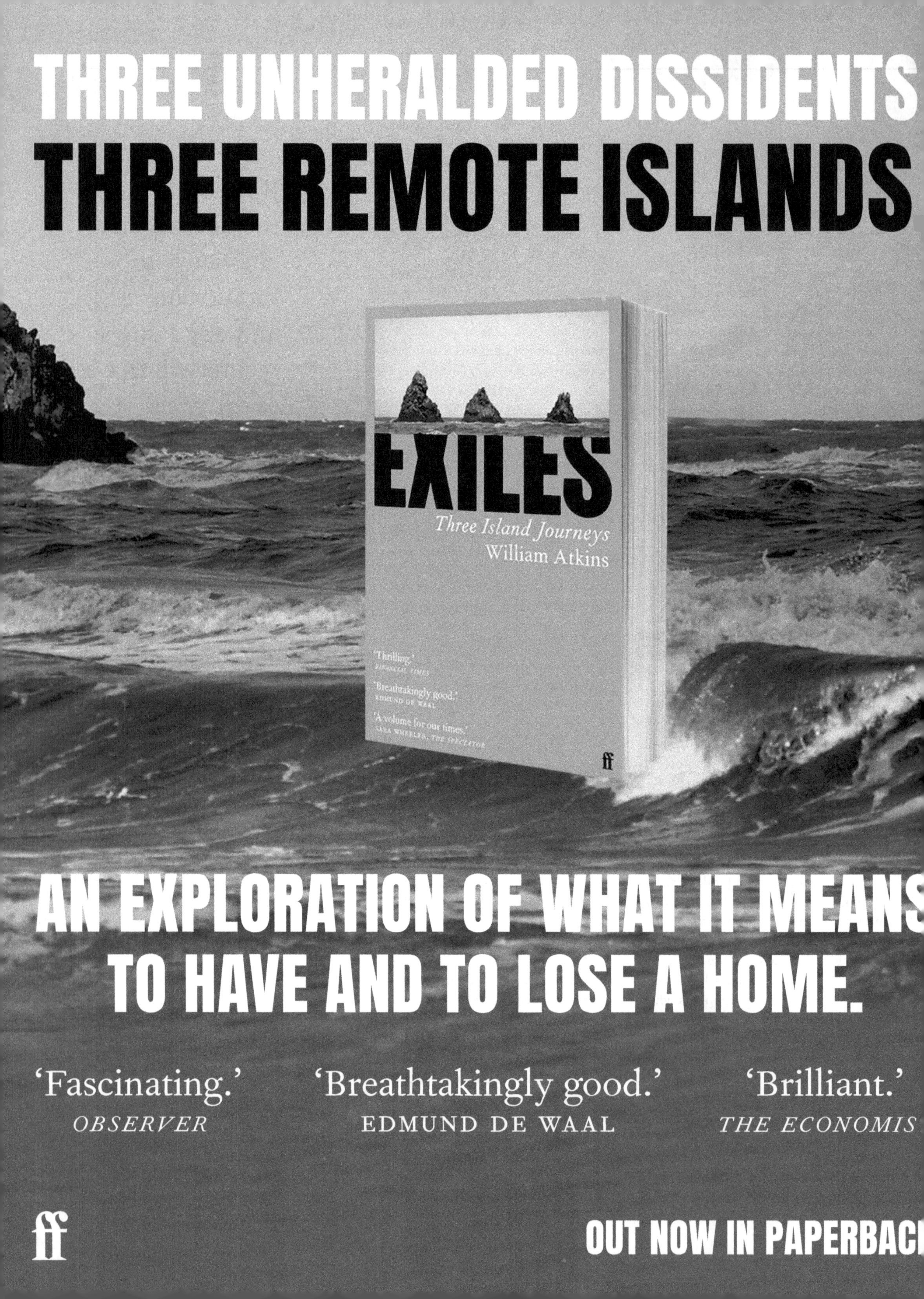
THREE UNHERALDED DISSIDENTS
THREE REMOTE ISLANDS
EXILES
Three Island Journeys
William Atkins
'Thrilling.'
'Breathtakingly good.'
'A volume for our times.'
AN EXPLORATION OF WHAT IT MEANS
TO HAVE AND TO LOSE A HOME.
'Fascinating.'
OBSERVER
'Breathtakingly good.'
EDMUND DE WAAL
'Brilliant.'
THE ECONOMIS
ff
OUT NOW IN PAPERBAC

COMMENT

"It was a new, collaborative way of doing journalism that challenged the way the United States conducted foreign policy"

SOLIDARITY, ASSANGE-STYLE | MARTIN BRIGHT | P.86

Solidarity, Assange-style

MARTIN BRIGHT opens up about his personal, complicated relationship with Julian Assange

I FIRST MET JULIAN Assange before he was Julian Assange. Or rather, when he was just becoming Julian Assange. For a few short months our fates were intertwined. And it all started with Index on Censorship.

In 2008, when I was political editor of the New Statesman, I was asked to collect an Index on Censorship New Media award on behalf of WikiLeaks, the organisation Assange founded two years earlier. I duly turned up for the event and was told the man himself had appeared at the caterers' entrance at the last-minute and my services would not be required. Secretive and not a little melodramatic, I soon discovered this was the way Assange liked to do business. The speech was impressive, expressing how much Assange valued solidarity and his admiration for "syndicalism", the belief that direct action can drive political change.

I wrote about that evening in my New Statesman blog and Assange noticed another item, where I discussed the newly aggressive approach the

LEFT: Julian Assange speaks to the media outside Belmarsh court in 2011

law firm Carter Ruck was taking with one of its clients, Nadhmi Auchi, an Iraqi billionaire convicted of fraud in France as part of the giant Elf-Aquitaine scandal. Mr Auchi continues to deny the charges. Newspapers who had written about Auchi's business dealings were being threatened with legal action if they didn't remove articles from their websites. Most of them eventually complied rather than face steep legal bills. Assange acted quickly to hoover up everything he could about Auchi and published it on WikiLeaks. It was a bold move because Carter Ruck were playing hardball. When I published a link to the Auchi files on my blog, the law firm threatened to sue the New Statesman.

I recently came across an email from Assange which he sent in November 2008, when he found out the New Statesman was planning to cave. He condemned the magazine for removing the original blogpost and objected to plans to issue a statement saying the articles collected by WikiLeaks (and published by respected journalists in national newspapers) contained significant inaccuracies. He pointed out that this action would in itself be defamatory.

This was solidarity and syndicalism, Assange-style. The New Statesman decided to settle with the billionaire, and I soon parted company with the magazine.

A few months later, a WikiLeaks emissary walked into the offices of a charity I had set up to help young people break into the creative industries on London's Southbank. He showed me footage of the 12 July 2007 Baghdad airstrike in which two Reuters journalists and several civilians were killed by a missile from a US helicopter. After a few further discussions, I advised him to talk to major news outlets about this extraordinary story. Shortly after this, WikiLeaks (in collaboration with The Guardian, The New York Times, Le Monde, Der Spiegel and El Pais) began publishing the US diplomatic cables that made Assange's reputation. It was a new, collaborative way of doing journalism that challenged the way the United States conducted foreign policy. Solidarity and syndicalism in action, perhaps.

We live in different times and Julian Assange finds himself in Belmarsh high-security prison awaiting the result of his final appeal against extradition to the United States, where he faces trial under the Espionage Act. In the interim, he has become a highly divisive figure and much of the solidarity from his former journalistic collaborators has evaporated. He has made serious errors of judgment and attracted some unfortunate allies. His radar for what constitutes genuine dissent has always been questionable. As former Index journalist Padraig Reidy pointed out in an important piece on Assange in BuzzFeed News in 2019: "Assange's definition of 'power' and 'elite' often stretched only as far as Western governments and their allies." Over the years, it has sometimes seemed that the principles of solidarity only worked in one direction. With each new twist in the story, a new layer of support dropped away. When Assange jumped bail and found refuge in London's Ecuadorian embassy, when he published hacked emails from Hilary Clinton's 2016 election campaign, when he suggested he was the victim of a conspiracy of Jewish journalists and was found to have employed a Holocaust denier, this all contributed to the picture of Assange as a narcissistic, paranoid self-publicist whose path was littered with the collateral damage of his overblown ego.

The question is whether it is possible to set all this aside and look at the bigger picture or if Assange's flaws and failings are an integral part of the bigger picture. Meanwhile, those journalists who have worked with him over the years need to ask themselves if his present predicament as a prisoner in the UK's highest security prison is just desserts or a travesty of justice.

The French free expression organisation, Reporters Without Borders, which has been consistent in its support for Assange, published a useful list of common misconceptions in the Assange case: that he is a traitor to the United States (he is Australian), that he leaked classified information (he published it), that he knowingly put people at risk (the prosecution has struggled to prove harm). But most powerful is the misconception that if he is convicted this will have no wider effect. There is already ample evidence that governments are determined to deter journalists from ever working with the likes of Assange again. The new UK National Security Act has specific measures to increase sentences for journalists working on data leak stories involving official secrets. Add to this the use of the US Espionage Act. Assange would be the first publisher tried under this act and if convicted he might not be the last.

Julian Assange is so wrong about so much. He has made many terrible mistakes. He is, in some ways, the agent of his own misfortune. But he taught journalists that some stories are so important that they need international collaboration to put them into the public domain. He was not wrong about the importance of solidarity. ✖

He is, in some ways, the agent of his own misfortune

Martin Bright is editor-at-large at Index

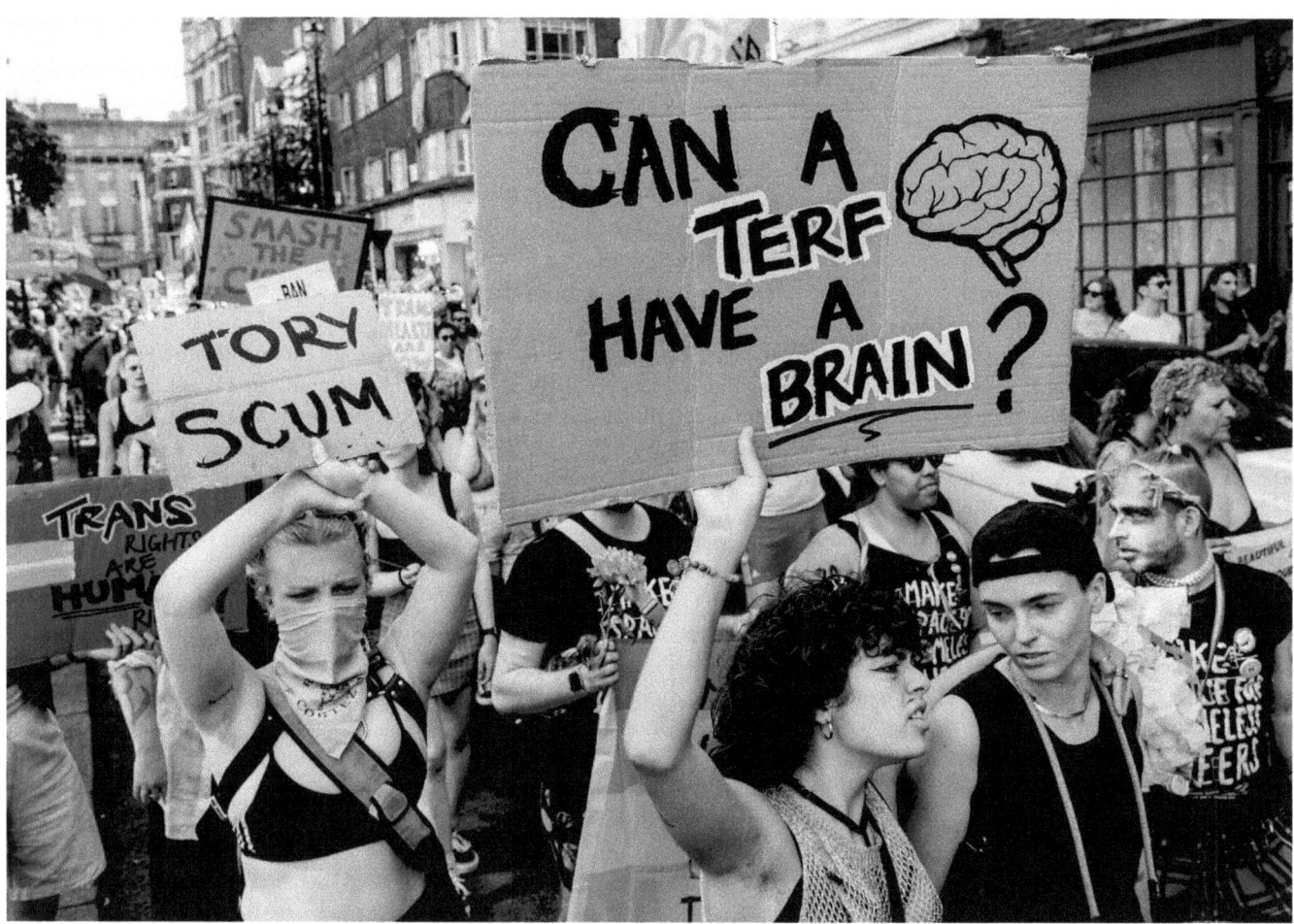

Challenging words

EMMA L BRIANT discusses the outcome of a recent case concerning academic freedom and what it could mean for some of today's most charged terms

IN A DECISION that could have a profound impact on universities throughout the UK, on 22 January criminology professor Jo Phoenix won her employment tribunal against the Open University over discrimination and harassment, which created a hostile environment that prevented her working. Gender-critical feminists such as Phoenix have made appeals to free speech, so it is ironic that the decision may result in more policing of speech – namely, that opposing gender-critical feminists.

In June 2021, Phoenix started a Gender Critical Research Network at the OU. This was met with a barrage of criticism and hate that became intolerable. Evidence presented at the Tribunal included moments like when a colleague likened Phoenix to "the racist uncle at the Christmas dinner table". There were online accusations of transphobia and a public letter calling for the network to be disaffiliated from the OU, which gained 360 signatures. Phoenix's evidence also highlighted union debates where colleagues argued research on subjects they considered discriminatory should not be permitted, comparing gender-critical feminism to Holocaust denial. Just without the genocide of Jews.

Not wishing to out-exaggerate these critics, the Phoenix decision has been followed by a supportive article by Professor Ian Pace of City, University of London, in Times Higher Education, in which he compares academic "mobbing" to the mass mobilisation of students against teachers under communism. Just without the communist state.

"Mobbing" tactics – such as pile-ons

LEFT: A London Trans+ Pride march in 2022. The use of labels such as "Terf" is now under the spotlight

in academic lists – are akin to trolling and can get ugly. But the ruling and the debate surrounding it raises important questions of what's acceptable speech, starting with: Is an open letter that successfully gathers signatures harassment?

Open letters to mobilise pressure behind social movements are common in academia and civil society. They have a long history, going back to the 19th century. I've signed them myself. Phoenix signed such letters: in 2018, one organised by another gender-critical feminist, Kathleen Stock gained 54 signatures and called for academic freedom and criticised close links between universities and trans-advocacy organisations. Another letter in 2021, signed by 600 people (not by Phoenix), protested Stock being made an OBE.

Most open letters have little effect on the institutions they hope to influence. Stock, for example, still became an OBE. But this open letter, combined with the other ways Phoenix was treated, culminated in her being instructed by her head of department not to speak about her research in her own department, which contributed to her being diagnosed with acute PTSD and becoming too unwell to work. In 2021, she began the process of bringing a constructive dismissal case against the OU for not protecting her against harassment in the workplace.

Gender-critical feminists like Phoenix have been arguing for academic freedom and the right to speak, but I would argue (as indeed would Phoenix) that should not bestow the right to speak unopposed, which is why it's worrying that in an interview Phoenix did in THE following the tribunal outcome, she highlighted how the decision "established the parameters within which debate can take place". She argues these new parameters could make the language of her critics – and that of activism, such as the words "transphobe" and "Terf" (trans-exclusionary radical feminist) – harassment. The ruling in part rested on an argument that the emotive open letter was not scholarly critique.

But in academia not all speech is spun in an ivory tower. James Murray, legal director at workplace law firm Doyle Clayton, recognises this nuance and lamented the "lack of critical reflection on what academic freedom actually is". In THE Phoenix echoes the conclusion the criticism was not "scholastic", comparing such words to calling someone "poo-face". I would argue to the contrary: while both may be insults, unlike "poo-face" the power words like "transphobe" have lies in their inherent critiques of ideology. Phoenix recognises this too when she argues this term is in the same realm as "racist", "homophobe" and "sexist" and intended to silence. Whether she likes the tone or not, it is the political critique within these words that is affronting – and there lies the very essence of academic freedom. These views should be debated in the classroom, yes, but this must include both sides, including some who may use such political speech.

In placing these words outside the parameters of acceptable speech we risk making it difficult for trans students and staff to confidently speak up about transphobia, for fear of being accused of harassment. Furthermore, the decision's shifting of the acceptable parameters of debate may create wider ripples across academia. If on this basis the use of the word "transphobe" is harassment, universities may find after this decision that they get cases where identifying someone as a homophobe, a racist, an antisemite or a sexist could similarly be challenged as harassment.

In recent years, following the UK's decline in academic freedom rankings, a Higher Education (Freedom of Speech) Act was introduced, and a new "Free Speech Tsar", Arif Ahmed, has pledged to defend "all views". Yet the parameters argument could move us in the wrong direction. Universities may be forced to retreat into euphemisms, but meaning rarely stays within the confines of forbidden language. New terms replace old. The term "Terf" was invented by the gender-critical feminist Viv Smythe as a neutral term. Through use, it became a slur, until finally it was replaced with another neutral descriptor – "gender critical". If avoiding accusations of harassment comes down to axing certain words, we may well find the meaning of today's permitted term "gender critical" changes through widespread disapproving use.

Whether or not one agrees with Phoenix on gender-critical theory, she undoubtedly suffered substantial trauma as a result of the months of harassment she experienced. Phoenix expected – and should have got – more support from her employer. It is also likely that open letters, protests, being deplatformed and union debates all helped feed the social media harassment machine, with the end result being Phoenix could not work. In today's social media environment, where fear and identity-driven divisive content is profitable in driving our engagement in the attention economy, hate speech has surged. This is experienced more acutely by women and minorities – including the trans community who themselves are swamped in constant hate speech as a result of real-world systematic denial of their rights. Phoenix has detailed similarly violent rhetoric used against those termed Terfs. Still, if it is social media that incentivises violent rhetoric and turns traditional forms of mobilisation, such as an open letter, in this new context into harassment then it is social media that must be reformed, not academic criticism that must be silenced. ✖

Emma L Briant is a leading expert on propaganda and information warfare, and associate professor in news and political communication at Monash University

GLOBAL VIEW

Good, bad and everything that's in between

The simple lens of good versus bad that dominated the Cold War is gone. Today censorship comes from all angles, even from the well-meaning, writes **RUTH ANDERSON**

WHEN THE FIRST edition of Index on Censorship was launched in 1972, the world was a very different place. Issues of free speech, democracy and liberty were looked at through a binary prism. Communists in the East and liberal democracies in the West. The role of Index was clear.

We provided a platform for dissidents in the Soviet Bloc and gave a voice to campaigners against tyranny. We ensured that inside the USSR the stories that needed to be told were heard and outside, we used our platform in the West to draw attention to the brutality that was taking place.

And while today, 52 years on, the role of Index remains clear, the world in which we operate is very different. The traditional Cold War divide that separated the champions of free speech from those seeking oppression is no longer as clearly defined. The clear-cut world of 'good' and 'bad' is now a sea of varying greys in which those seeking silence are often the self-proclaimed saviours of free speech. The advent of social media and clickbait commentators has created a whole new digital realm in which hate speech can be dressed up as free speech and where 'pile-ons' are frequent and considered debate is rare.

And whereas the frontline in the 70s and 80s was the threat of incarceration and death for those who speak out against tyranny, there exists a whole new series of weapons in the arsenal of people wielding the weapon of censorship.

Of course the threats of the old world are still there. The recent unexplained death of Alexei Navalny while in a Russian prison is a sad reminder that despots who seek to hold power will use every possible tool to do so. Likewise, the continuing show trial of Jimmy Lai in Hong Kong shines a light on the abuse of power against those who speak out in defence of free speech and a free press.

But what is also emerging is the pro-active silencing of opinion in the new frontiers of free speech.

The use of social media to hound companies and venues to cease their partnerships with individuals or celebrities who voice their opinions is all too common. So is the targeting of venues that become sites of protests or subject to thousands of social media comments because they host an organisation or individual who holds views or opinions contrary to the detractors.

Cancel culture and a subsequent climate of self-censorship is as common a threat to freedom of expression today as the barbarity of the Soviet Union was in the 70s and 80s. In a world which now sees more people live under dictatorships than democracies, it is increasingly disappointing to see those who have the right to free speech using that right to silence others.

The growing intolerance between differing opinions is creating a vitriolic space in which dominance of opinion, backed by almost unwavering certainty of moral righteousness, is forcing out moderate and nuanced voices in favour of those who can shout the loudest with the simplest and easiest digestible slogans. Whether through trying to take away their jobs, have them de-platformed or labelled as social pariahs for daring to carry an alternative opinion, the impact on those people is all too real and it is becoming increasingly common.

And the consequence is that self-censorship is the route chosen by those who fear speaking their mind on contested or controversial topics. The thought unsaid or the opinion unspoken through fear – not always of physical attack but of a concerted attempt by organised groups to delegitimise individuals – is reducing the number of voices that take part in discussions. The tone of our public space is all the poorer for it.

Social media companies themselves also have questions to answer. They decide, via methods which are often opaque, who is and who isn't allowed to have a platform, who is and isn't allowed to speak and in some cases their algorithms also determine who can be heard. The result is debates dominated by the appeal of clickbait rather than content.

This can be compounded by well-meaning attempts by governments freely and fairly elected who choose to regulate the online spaces and in a series of unintended consequences can create even more tools for censorship. In an attempt to create a level playing-field in our democratic pursuits and temper what are considered to be the darkest and bleakest recesses of the digital world, these blunt tools see legitimate campaigners and content silenced and removed.

We are guided to content that social media thinks we want to see. In democratic societies, I believe this content moderation is done with good intent - whether it is protecting children or protecting our mental health - but it can lead to a bubble in which views different to our own or questions posed to deliberately start debate are side-lined in

ABOVE: Flowers are left by a mural of George Floyd in Denver, Colorado

favour of the comfort of reaffirming our own view point at the expense of others.

It's not the traditional censorship of the USSR but nevertheless it is censorship. Unseen, unspoken and often unknown.

The flip-side, of course, is that the almost constant documentation of our lives, current events and news as a result of social media, citizen journalism and grassroot campaigning can change world events almost immediately. The most obvious example is the horrendous murder of George Floyd, the recording of which led to a global anti-racist movement challenging the status quo. This is also one of the reasons why autocratic regimes actively seek to turn off social media when they do not want their own citizens knowing what they are doing.

At the heart of this debate is where does freedom of expression fit and who are the good guys in a world increasingly challenged by propaganda, misinformation and conspiracy? Where is the time for analysis, for debate and for nuance in a world driven by clickbait, which impacts even the most robust media agencies?

In what feels like an increasingly divided world, how are clickbait commentators and the occasional ignorance of well-intended campaigners challenged without censoring? Or rather leading to a social media storm targeting either the commentator or the challenge? When misinformation and propaganda become normal and debatable, how do you counteract it without simply shutting it down or censoring the messenger? When our bad faith actors or the spokespeople for terror groups, despotic totalitarians and dictators are addressing the world through the internet with fantastical messages which are devoid of truth and paint a fictitious picture of their own supposed martyrdom, what approach do we take that doesn't deny them their right to free expression? How then can we champion freedom of expression while seeking to take on tyranny when those tyrants themselves now deploy their own freedoms as weapons against others?

I pose these questions not because I know the answer but because as we move forward in an increasingly dangerous world in which alliances for freedoms are no longer binary and where international collaborations put a strain on the supposedly settled international institutions, the new frontiers of freedoms require a new approach to their protections. ✖

Ruth Anderson is Index CEO

These blunt tools see legitimate campaigners and content silenced

45 contemporary Kurdish women poets, including

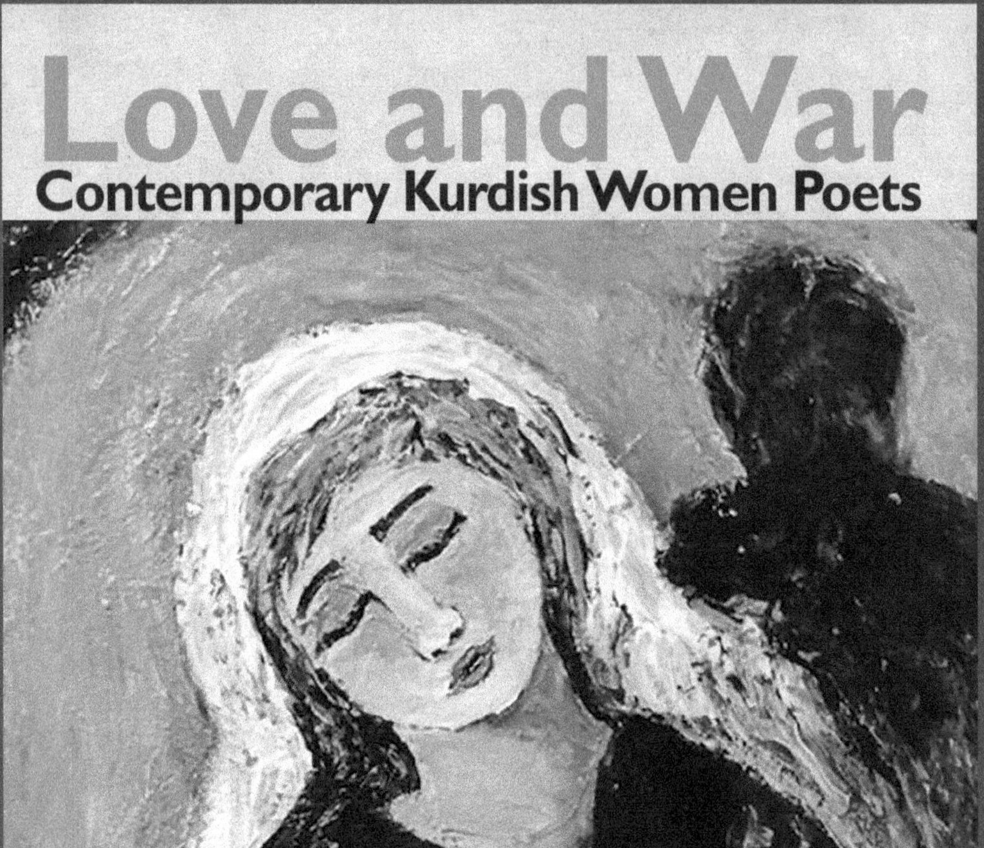

Bejan Matur

Avin Shakaki,

Fadwa Kilani

and

Sînîn Çaycî.

ISBN: 9781739734268

Price: £9.99

Smokestack Books
www.smokestack-books.co.uk

CULTURE

"And the war is here now, in the room. With the features of a fascist occupier, with the arm patches of evil on its dirty uniform"

UKRAINE'S DISAPPEARING INK | STEPHEN KOMARNYCKYJ & VICTORIA AMELINA | P.94

Ukraine's disappearing ink

At the age of 37, novelist, poet and human rights activist **VICTORIA AMELINA**'s life was brutally terminated. **STEPHEN KOMARNYCKYJ** introduces a new translation of one of her short stories

I WROTE TO VICTORIA Amelina, who I did not know personally, on 8 May 2023 to invite her to participate in Stanzas for Ukraine, a series of blogs by Ukrainian poets I was producing for The Poetry School. She responded promptly with a selection of poems, and promised to write a blog. We also spoke about an anthology of short stories by Ukrainian authors I am compiling for Dedalus Books, and she sent me two tales – one of which, The Nameless, I present here.

The story is a vignette from the war with a dash of magic realism and a twist. A little girl hides in a cupboard as a soldier roams around her room. Her readers would have assumed that the girl was Ukrainian and the soldier Russian, but there is a twist.

I was still waiting for the blog when Amelina was killed by a Russian missile strike on a restaurant in Kramatorsk on 27 June, although with characteristic tenacity she held on to life until 1 July. There was also a missile strike on Kremenchuk on the same day, presumably to "celebrate" the anniversary of Russia's missile strike on the Amstor shopping centre in the same city, which killed at least 20 people. Another poet who features in Stanzas for Ukraine, Alisa Havrylchenko, lives near the city, and I wrote several emails to her. My relief when she replied confirming that she had not been near the site of the explosion was short-lived. I found out later that Amelina had been injured and I hoped to the end that she would recover.

At the time, Amelina was working on a non-fiction project, Looking at Women Looking at War: War and Justice Diary. An award-winning prose author, whose work includes the novels Dom's Dream Kingdom and Fall Syndrome, she also founded the New York Literature Festival, which took place in a village called New York in the Bakhmut area.

Amelina is one of several Ukrainian poets to have died during the war. Many of the poets in the Stanzas for Ukraine series have narrowly avoided Russian missile and drone strikes, or are in the armed forces. One poet carried a note in her pocket in the early days of the war to allow her to be identified if Russian saboteurs should murder her. Russia's aim is to eradicate the notion of a distinct Ukrainian national culture, and the damage inflicted on the country's literature and arts is central to a war that Moscow is using as an instrument of cultural erasure.

Amelina was very aware that the war was a continuation of last century's genocide in Ukraine, which caused millions of deaths through famine, along with targeted killings, including those of prominent authors. This is why the murder of the writer Volodymyr

ABOVE: The award-winning Ukrainian novelist Victoria Amelina, who was killed in the summer of 2023 by a Russian missile strike while she was eating in a restaurant

Vakulenko, who was killed when his village, Izium in Kharkiv Oblast, was occupied by Russian soldiers in 2022, was so significant for her.

From 2022 onwards, Amelina collaborated with Ukrainian NGOs, including Truth Hounds and the Centre for Civil Liberties, to document war crimes and advocate for accountability for the international crimes committed in Ukraine. In an essay for PEN Ukraine, she summarised her situation and that of her fellow poets and artists facing yet another round of culling by Russia:

"Before the full-scale invasion, when the threat was already in the air, I kept thinking about Ukraine's Executed Renaissance. In the 1930s, the Soviet-Russian regime murdered the majority of Ukrainian writers and intellectuals. The few that survived were scared and unfree. And this, of course, wasn't the first time the Ukrainian elite had been erased or forced to assimilate to Russian imperial culture.

"The purges and centuries of unimaginable pressure are why you don't often hear about great Ukrainian literature, theatre and art. When you look at the map of Europe, you see Dante here and Shakespeare [there], but only a vast gap where Ukrainian culture should have been to make Europe whole and safe.

"Now there is a real threat that Russians will successfully execute another generation of Ukrainian culture – this time by missiles and bombs."

There are, indeed, Ukrainian

> One poet carried a note in her pocket in the early days of the war to allow her to be identified if Russian saboteurs should murder her

equivalents of Dante and Shakespeare, and returning them to the world's cultural heritage is part of overcoming, in so far as is possible, Russia's historic genocide. However, Ukrainian literature remains marginalised and its creators were murdered and destroyed in their hundreds. As Amelina also noted in her essay, the Russians destroyed the second manuscript of Mykola Khvylovy's short story The Woodsnipes and every copy of the magazine where it appeared. It is not an isolated incident: many manuscripts by Ukrainian authors were destroyed and many of them never wrote the books they might have written because they were repressed or murdered.

Time will tell if we care enough to stop the erasure of Ukrainian culture and another expansion of Russia that wipes a whole people off the map to make lands completely Russian, as is the case in places such as Adygea and Buryatia. The mentality that led to the severing of human heads in the Caucasus of the 19th century has survived intact through repeated genocides: Vladimir Putin says that Russia has no borders and Alexander Pushkin spoke of the war with Poland as a "war of extermination". His words resemble those that have been spoken of Ukraine by many contemporary Russian authors, but the question for us is where we set a boundary on the role of Russian literature and the cultural erasure many of its canonical texts normalise, and on the country's physical expansion. Surely the death of yet another great Ukrainian author will finally compel us to realise that Ukrainians are fighting a war that is our war also and they are shielding Europe from an unsated imperialism. That would be a fitting tribute to Victoria Amelina.

Stephen Komarnyckyj is a British-Ukrainian award-winning poet and translator

The Nameless Ones

By **VICTORIA AMELINA**

THE APERTURE IS long and intensely bright like that rim of light the sun leaves in its wake before completely surrendering to the darkness. So, the front line must also surely disappear before the tortuous occupation. Her breath will give her away and lose her her head. That fair-haired head with the pigtails still untwined from yesterday. Quieter! Oh quieter Nadia. You must become a little mouse, a grey no one the size of a teeny pebble and then you will be able to flee, run through the arid fields, vaulting, almost flying over the dunes, bypassing father's slag-heaps. It isn't difficult, it could still be done. How can it be that such a small thing as she was could breathe so loudly, loud as only the factory's horn sounded before.

How has this happened? You woke up at dawn, put a party dress on, unearthed your favourite toy, the one with the big ears, which your grandma confiscated for disobedience, took out a rotund jar of apricot jam, brilliant amber like the beads also found in the drawer, along with your father's photo. Your father had to have tea with you and Vukhatyi, Big Ears, eating jam with a big spoon, that only you would eat now, but your dad would watch as if he was happy for you. What to do now? You rummage in the closet and that aperture, slender and bright, shows everything, as was only seen before on TV, that is terrifying: everything that grandmother, old war movies and blokes from the televisions warned you about.

You heard how the floorboard creaked. Creaked quietly, and quietly and odiously just once. But memory suddenly dumped everything on you. Everything that you remembered even though it had not happened to you: all that you had seen on the television, that those blokes had seen with their own eyes, everything that Grandma had heard on the market and from the neighbours. And how you crawled into the closet and banged your knee, which now hurts in the darkness and probably, oh such rotten rotten luck, will stain your clothes red (and fly from Grandma), how you hid behind an old fur coat, which you were afraid of because it was from some scary fanged beast. The girl had forgotten the creature's name.

And now she breathes heavily, and the fur of this nameless creature hides her from the war, as people now use blankets to hide from the shelling. And the war is here now, in the room. With the features of a fascist occupier, with the arm patches of evil on its dirty uniform. And how much Nadia hates now! And how much it now transpires that you can hate. You are able to hate and want to hate. The tears come and the damp makes that coat smell of the scary creature. And such sorrow for herself she has, this little one guilty of nothing and so pretty in a party dress.

* * *

The Commander was utterly destroyed, in burned clothes, but somehow intact. He fell through the entrance into the house that, from a distance, resembled his grandmother Nastya's home. However, his grandmother remained back there, further to the North, merging into the earth that she loved so much after she died twenty years ago. That soil, strewn with pine needles, had pleasantly prickled her grandson's heels, but this soil here burns under his feet. The house is similar to Grandmother's house but also foreign, the soil is like his native soil but unforested, broken with slag-heaps which like pyramids draw their dead to themselves. The pillows in the house are, as they should be, stacked and covered with a translucent snow-white mesh, the television opposite the oven is a cathode-ray tube one, the Electrode brand. There are red carpets on the wooden floor as in a mausoleum. There is no icon in the corner. He thought about that and came round. One. Two, three… he forgot how many there were. The first, the second one… The first was Kolya, a lad with an invisible moustache, he kept growing it, but his efforts were pointless. His bristles, light as his skin, remained imperceptible when he fell on his back. And then they all understood (or was it only he, the Commander, who understood it all?): the enemy had seen them. Don't go out. Don't slither away. Do not become part of yet another necessary marvel that would be created for them with the times of this ungodly war. The first, the second, that was Sasha, whose call sign was…

"Lord!"

The Commander who had remained whole fell and crawled on his knees across those boards fashioned from distant pines, to that corner where the Madonna and child would hang in another house.

* * *

Through that slit, thin as the line of last light before the darkness, wiping with her sleeve tears, snot, hairs of that beast with its name forgotten, like entrails, that girl whose grandmother went to collect her pitiful pennies pension and never returned saw a horrific thing. Someone blackened with death was wandering around her room. A brute. He peered, listened, sniffed, although he resembled a dog, a werewolf. It was a miracle that he did not hear the girl's rasped breath, while he turned his huge bestial head silently and ran his dirty hands along the white walls. Then he stiffened suddenly and grimaced, as if a tooth ached; perhaps even a brute was afraid of the huge spider in the corner of the room. He fell to his knees, sobbed and howled as a wolf howls at the moon, at the spider webs on the ceiling. He stayed on his knees for a long time, as if he too were punishing himself where Nadia would be forced by her grandmother to kneel on dried peas for the slightest transgression.

But then – had he even heard her? – he looked at the closet. As if he saw Nadia and her jam through that gap. He stiffened and looked with his stupid eyes and Nadia understood completely now; this was the end. Then the brute rushed, covering the distance between them in a second, she closed her eyes and screamed, thought that she was screaming, and the silence rang in her ears and the blows thudded dully like a giant heart pounding in a place of utter silence. The closet shuddered because the pine boards on which the tiny victim lay ran through the whole room.

Bang! Bang! The killer delivered the blows raising his hand high and mumbling bestially. As if he wanted to kill all that lived in the whole world. And not just the little doll with the big ears and soft belly that he was smacking.

The killer stopped. He looked around as if

seeing the room for the first time. He wept. Wept long and bitterly rubbing the black grime from his face with his sleeve. Then he began rummaging through Grandmother's closets. There was a clink as a transparent bottle was sat on the table. Nadia thought he would kill her, only drink his fill and kill her, that happened a lot in their village even without the war.

But that moment passed. The brute drank and roared and calmed and became human. Finally he laid down on his side next to the maimed animal toy as if to meet the gaze of those plastic eyes and just fell asleep. He slept for a long time. Darkness was falling and the gap through which she viewed the room disappeared into the murk, taking the war with it. The girl lay down on her grandmother's cardigans, wrapped herself in them and, exhausted, fell asleep. She dreamed of lovely cartoons whose colours slowly faded until they became black and white, similar to Soviet cinema where undefeated people filmed in black and white perish one after another. And the sun was fading all this time and then out of nowhere it reappeared in the same place as yesterday, opposite that narrow gap between the doors of the closet.

During the day the brute drank and wept. Wept and drank. He switched on the TV, people spoke the truth. The girl knew this because the brute knocked the TV off its stand. The unprotected screen cracked and Nadia, even if she lived, would not see her big-eared friend again, even in a cartoon. And moreover the brute had eaten all the jam. Except for the last jar which remained in the palms of her hands. Tightly screwed shut.

→ And more than jam, even, she wanted something to drink and finally to emerge from the smelly sticky rags. Sweat coursed down her cheeks and Nadia smeared her fingers through it, licking her own sweat salty palms as if they were ice cream. And the sun slid its beam on the floor as if it too wanted to lick the deep wounds of her toy Cheburashka.

The killer squinted. He had neither drunk nor wept today. Maybe the bottle he drank yesterday was the last. And in a moment Nadia stopped being afraid, perhaps her thirst became greater than her fear. She wanted to cry but the tears would not come and then she too howled like a werewolf, albeit a small mouse-sized one.

* * *

"Who are you? Where are you from?"

The last light struck Nadia's face as she whispered "I am Nadia" and then added, for some reason, "from Novorossiia".

But of course that was not exactly what he wanted to ask, he only wanted to know where she had come from before she was in the wardrobe and Nadia wanted to die as a hero and not even a heroine. Like those brave blokes would have done on the TV. Nadia knew what she was going to do, and it was all about that big-eared doll with the white hole in its toy belly.

So the girl didn't flee, she was ready to lay her head with its two completely messed up pigtails on the chopping block. The brute stroked her dishevelled parting for a long while. He said something that was recognisable as language and raised a mug of water to his lips. Then, anxious that he had eaten all the foodstuffs in the house he began rifling through numerous drawers.

"I still have a jar of jam. Over there in the closet."

* * *

He pulled the table up to the window, brushing the crumbs from it with his sleeve, found the last of the teabags, finally washed the remaining grime from hands blackened with death and washed his face.

They drank tea in silence. The brute did not eat anything. He just watched how the girl ravenously scooped up the jam in a large spoon as if he were happy for her. She suddenly pushed the jar away as if she did not want to eat at the same table as him and didn't even want any more jam.

He was silent waiting for her to respond for a while, perhaps by screams, hysterics, running away. But the girl asked quietly: "Why do you hate Earie so much?"

Something cracked in the Commander as the TV screen had cracked earlier, breaking him in half.

"I really love him very much."

"Why did you then...?" the girl asks looking into his eyes.

This is how it will be at the Last Judgment. Just like this, the Commander thinks. Adults will be judged by children: why did you kill my Cheburashka?

The Commander was silent for a moment. How can he explain it? The past, that is yours. You are that past. You can never explain yourself. Your memories, of childhood with the flavour of barberry candies, a cartoon where a Cheburashka learns to march in formation, following behind the pioneers, the pioneers such as you. A childhood steeped with belief. They say that a generation had to pass. The Commander really longed to have passed already. But someone had given the girl, Nadia, a virus. Along with that little creature with the big ears...

"I love him and everything that brings us all..." He counted them again, the first was Kolya, the second Sasha, the third... it was possible to return to the past.

He says something more about the USSR, the way Soviet people were brought up, and the old propaganda of that belief and that war. The girl looks at him as if she were not breathing, as if she also had plastic eyes. She will probably not understand, say or ask anything. She only knows of the Soviet Union from that lamp monstrosity, whose fragments he had thrown out of the garden. But you cannot throw yourself out of the garden.

"All this because of Cheburashka?" the girl asks.

The enamelled mug clinks on the table and the sound of a train comes from somewhere else. They look into each other's eyes, an adult from the USSR who believes that he lives in Ukraine and a girl from Ukraine who believes that she lives in Novorossiia.

"Because," it was hard for him to say, "not because of Cheburashka. It's all because of me. Generally everything is because of me."

* * *

They didn't talk about Cheburashka any more. The man began sorting things in the house while grumbling: "What kind of a grandmother do you have, she hasn't even hung up the net curtain." Then he waved his hand and they drank tea, by the bare window with a view over the field and those paternal slag-heaps. They patched up the Cheburashka's cotton belly and sewed the ears back on but its smile had become a little crooked. The Commander was a poor hand at sewing and Nadia was too little to sew properly. Then he said, quietly and uncertainly, that after the war he would buy a new television for them. And he thought how naming a child Nadia, or Hope, was the same as not naming them at all because all children embody some hope.

But then he will probably also name his daughter Nadia sooner or later.

"I will soon be leaving."

"Where will you go?"

"An officer who has been surrounded must get back to his own side."

It was as if he was repeating something learned from a textbook. But he stopped himself.

"However, I can't get back to our side here. And if it is not possible to make it back to your own side, it is necessary simply to..."

"To what?"

"To continue fighting."

→ "But if you go I will be alone."

The Commander is silent, turning his case to the bare window which lacks a net curtain.

"Maybe you could just not go anywhere?"

* * *

They sat and drank tea by the window: the still relatively young Commander without a platoon, the bright girl from a non-existent country, and that strange creature with its scars, the nameless one. Because if it is the case that you do not know your own name, they would give you the most absurd one from all the possible names… is that really better than the total absence of a name?

They both watched as the sun sank behind the slag-heaps and sipped tea from enamel mugs with chipped rims and talked about some vacant topic. The Commander smiled. Shells flew above the little building that resembled his grandmother Nastya's house. Noiselessly as birds, not impacting anyone. So the Commander, the girl and the Cheburashka are already able to believe that things had to be this way. And would always be so.

Perhaps, the Commander thought, the shells would pass him and Nadia by because they are, quite simply, no longer in this world.

The girl wonders if, perhaps, they should never have been here.

Perhaps, the Cheburashka thinks, it will occur to these two one day to put yet another, third mug on the table, but the doll, like the people, is silent. Most importantly the troops had stopped shooting around them for now and maybe it was better that everyone thought the Cheburashka was dead.

Somewhere, in the real world, the sun rises at last. ✖

Victoria Amelina was an award-winning Ukrainian novelist. Translated by Stephen Komarnyckyj

CULTURE

One-way ticket to freedom?

The Saudi government is trying to break the spirit of **GHANEM AL MASARIR**, but he is not silenced yet. He spoke to **JEMIMAH STEINFELD** after writing a comedy script for Index

WITHIN A FEW hours of Ghanem al Masarir accepting the invitation to perform at Index's January comedy night – an event centred on dissent – the Saudi satirist had sent over a script of what he wanted to say.

It was great – funny, pacey and laced with on-the-nose jokes about Saudi's Crown Prince that you'd want from a dissident. The only problem was it was a bit short for his allocated timeslot. Could he expand it?

His reply was to pull out of the event entirely. He told me his mental health was in such a state that he didn't think he could do it. We'd spoken in the morning, a time when he typically feels more robust. By the afternoon he'd been having doubts and was concerned that, as per his current pattern, he'd be unable to muster the strength to perform at a night-time event. My request for a bit more bulk tipped him over the edge.

Al Masarir's message was disappointing, but it was not unpredictable. The Saudi authorities →

INDEXONCENSORSHIP.ORG **101**

I heard the Saudi government is introducing a new reality show. It's called Dissidence Island. Contestants compete to see who can question authority the longest without disappearing

→ have been terrorising him for years, in a way that is intended to destroy his mental, as much as his physical, health.

He arrived in the UK in 2003 when he came to study. He was in his early 20s and had no intention to stay, but while he was here he encountered Saudi opposition – a fact that made its way back to Saudi authorities who, in al Masarir's words, went crazy.

"They wanted to make my life miserable. If you visit Osama bin Laden they're fine with that, but not if you visit opposition," he told Index.

Al Masarir said the harassment took the form of trying to discredit his reputation and thereby limit his professional opportunities, as well as illegal actions such as stealing his car (it apparently later showed up in Dubai) and hacking his bank account.

His first job was recruiting students

ABOVE: Dissident comic Ghanem al Masarir continues to speak out against the Saudi regime despite being mentally worn down by their harassment campaign

from the Middle East to study in the UK, something he was driven out of after several people he recruited were themselves threatened.

In 2015, al Masarir turned his hand to comedy. He set up a YouTube channel on which he'd post satirical videos, talk show-host style, about the Saudi state. The videos were watched by tens of thousands, mostly from Saudi Arabia – a testament to the hunger in the country for this kind of content ("black messages", as al Masarir calls them), which he thought would be more effective in their messaging than more formal content.

Throughout this time al Masarir was still in contact with his family. That ended in 2017 following a campaign where he called on people in Saudi Arabia to upload their own videos (which some did, using VPNs to protect themselves). The Saudi authorities promptly pressured his family to cut ties and he hasn't spoken to any of them since – an obviously painful fact, and one that he says he tries not to think about too much in a bid to stay positive.

I wanted to meet al Masarir, to speak to him face to face. But he is evasive. Then he tells me he rarely leaves his London home.

"I used to go to Hyde Park to walk around. I'd meet people in the city centre. Now I don't," he said.

In 2018, al Masarir was outside Harrods in central London when he was badly beaten by men who, it is believed, were hired by the Saudi state. (Citizen Lab confirmed that his phone had been hacked using Pegasus spyware.)

While al Masarir was lucky to get away without anything broken, the same could not be said of his spirit. "They destroyed me emotionally," he said.

"The UK is a great country and everything is amazing, but I think the UK is too close to the Saudis. You run away from the evil Saudis and they can reach you in the West."

At the same time, they destroyed him financially, blocking his videos in Saudi Arabia and asking YouTube on occasion to take them down. He said they obliged.

Al Masarir must have had a morsel of strength left, though, because in 2022 he made the unprecedented move of suing the Kingdom of Saudi Arabia in the UK for hacking his phone and for the 2018 assault. He won the case, only to have the Saudis appeal it a year later. They lost, and today al Masarir is awaiting the outcome of the damages they owe him, and he hopes to get what he deserves for what they've done to him.

Is there a number that can be put on that? The short answer is "No".

"I'm now 43. I've lost the best years of my life. I don't think I can get that back," he said.

His case could help other hacking victims in the UK sue foreign governments who order similar attacks, and thereby dissuade those governments from such conduct.

"I hope it sends a message to not commit these sorts of crimes in a sovereign country. Saudi should not be allowed to do what they have done," al Masarir said.

On the day of the Index event, my phone buzzes. It's al Masarir sending over an extra part for the script. He still doesn't have the strength to perform on stage, but the fact that he can write it – and that he wants others to see it – is something.

The Saudi state has taken so much from al Masarir, but it hasn't totally removed his voice. In him lies hope.

Jemimah Steinfeld is editor-in-chief at Index

Having the last laugh: A celebration of dissidence

HEY, EVERYBODY! HOW'S it going tonight? Good? Awesome! So, I've been thinking a lot about dissidence lately. You know, the art of going against the grain, challenging the status quo, and basically being a rebel with a cause. Or without a cause. Because, let's be honest, sometimes rebellion is its own cause, right?

I mean, who here has ever disagreed with something just for the sake of it? Come on, raise your hands. Yeah, that's what I'm talking about. Dissidence is like the rebellious teenager of adulthood. It's that little voice in your head saying: "Hey, why not take the road less travelled? It might have better snacks."

I recently had this realisation that dissidence is like a muscle. The more you use it, the stronger it gets. And sometimes it gets so strong that you find yourself questioning everything. I questioned my morning coffee once. I asked it: "Are you really the best part of waking up, or is that just a catchy jingle?"

You ever notice how dissidence has its own soundtrack? Like, rebellion comes with its own playlist. The moment you decide to go against the flow, suddenly punk rock becomes your theme music. I once played Anarchy in the UK while doing my taxes. It didn't make them more enjoyable, but at least I felt like a financial maverick.

Of course, with dissidence comes critics. People who just can't handle you breaking the mould. I had someone tell me: "Why are you always going against the grain?"

I said: "Have you tried the other side of the bread? It's pretty delicious."

But hey, dissidence is not for everyone. It's an acquired taste, like cilantro or political debates at Thanksgiving.

You know who the real rebels are? People who assemble furniture without reading the instructions. They're out there, living on the edge, defying the laws of Swedish design. And let me tell you, that's a rebellion I can get behind. Screw you, Allen key!

Speaking of defying expectations, did you hear about Mohammed bin Salman's visit to the UK? They were so worried about him carrying a bone-saw that they installed metal detectors at Buckingham Palace. Turns out, the Queen wasn't a fan of impromptu home improvements.

But hey, let's not be too hard on them. Maybe they just wanted to make sure he wasn't planning a surprise visit to the Tower of London gift shop.

And speaking of surprises, have you caught wind of the new Saudi Arabian cooking show? It's called Dissident Chef. Contestants compete to make the most revolutionary dish without getting censored... The winner gets a lifetime supply of olive oil and a free subscription to Cooking in Exile magazine.

They say the secret ingredient is dissent, but good luck finding that in the spice aisle.

You know you're in Saudi Arabia when the government hires GPS for its dissidents. "In 500 metres, make a U-turn to the nearest detention centre. Failure to comply may result in unexpected travel plans to a place with less Wi-Fi."

I heard the Saudi government is introducing a new reality show. It's called Dissidence Island. Contestants compete to see who can question authority the longest without disappearing. Spoiler alert: the winner gets a one-way ticket to Freedom Island – also known as exile.

In conclusion, let's celebrate dissidence. Embrace your inner rebel, question the norms and remember that, sometimes, the best way to have the last laugh is by being the one who laughs first. Cheers to the misfits, the contrarians and the ones who refuse to colour inside the lines!

Thank you, everyone! You've been a fantastic crowd. And remember, if life gives you lemons, make dissident lemonade. Goodnight! ✖

Ghanem al Masarir is a Saudi dissident satirist and activist based in the UK

The show must go on

A theatre company based in the Jenin refugee camp operates under the most testing circumstances and since the Israel-Gaza escalation their fight for freedom of all kinds has never been more vital. **KATIE DANCEY-DOWNS** speaks to their head of acting **YASMIN SAMEER**

THE FREEDOM THEATRE in the Palestinian West Bank was preparing for a full rehearsal of its latest production Big Love by US playwright Charles L Mee. The play tackles feminism, society and freedom and is the story of 50 brides who run away from marrying their cousins. For the world-renowned theatre company based in the Jenin refugee camp, this would have been another production pushing boundaries, but it was not to be. The day of that rehearsal was 7 October 2023.

As the full extent of what had happened became clear, the head of the acting school Yasmin Sameer thought, "Ok, maybe we are in a war." She went back to be with her family in Jerusalem. Sameer was right. The Hamas attack on Israel, the retaliatory air strikes on Gaza and subsequent ground invasion by the Israeli army were the latest events in a long 75 year history of occupation and resistance, and there would be a knock-on effect on the West Bank.

While the eyes of the world were further south, the West Bank was locked down, roads closed and movement restricted. Incursions by Israeli forces were launched into cities. Rehearsals, and indeed the tour which should have started a few weeks later, never came.

"It was way too much to think about anything else," Sameer remembers about the following weeks, when theatre staff and students were separated. They struggled to communicate. After a few weeks, Sameer made the decision to start

PICTURED: A rehearsal at the Freedom Theatre in Jenin, in the West Bank, July 2020

running Zoom classes for her students.

"Some days we had to stop because of an invasion of a certain city," Sameer told Index. "It is hard to make art in the midst of all of this. Especially

We believe that if you want to be free, you need your society also to be free

CREDIT: Raneen Sawafta/Reuters

> One, she said, was beaten by Israeli soldiers for not having Instagram on their phone at all, with the assumption they must have deleted the app to hide something

→ theatre. Theatre is such a physical thing that you really miss a lot when you do it in another way. And when you are in the middle of the trauma [...] it's hard for you to articulate what you're feeling."

The Freedom Theatre prides itself on its courageous output, with a mission of cultural resistance. In February 2024, the theatre was nominated for a Nobel Peace Prize.

Sameer said: "We believe that if you want to be free, you need your society also to be free. To tackle more sensitive stuff, to talk about it more freely: women's rights to decide, freedom of speech to say what you believe freely without having to worry about it. And we are also a conservative community, so we have also these challenges."

Sameer explains that they believe in resisting every kind of oppression: "That's why we talk a lot about feminism, that's why we talk about freedom of speech, that's why we talk about the freedom of Palestine, which is the main thing."

After weeks of online classes following the outbreak of war, Sameer and her students felt they needed to be back in the theatre. "When they invade… we will stop," they decided.

It wasn't long before that happened. Sameer was at her home in Jerusalem on 13 December 2023 when Jenin was raided by Israeli forces.

"They were in the theatre, destroying and sabotaging things," Sameer said. "Jenin and the refugee camp is often invaded and often there is destruction, but that particular day was really, really hard."

A message came in from a colleague: Mustafa Sheta, the theatre's general manager, had been arrested from his apartment in Jenin City. Only an hour or so later, Sameer remembers, artistic director Ahmed Tobasi was also arrested, followed shortly by Freedom Theatre graduate and acting trainer Jamal Abu Joas.

Arts and human rights organisations around the world, including Index, Pen International and London's Royal Court Theatre, called for their release. Tobasi and Abu Joas were released later in the week, but Sheta has reportedly been sentenced to six months in administrative detention, imprisoned without charge. Sameer said they have no contact with him.

After the raid, some students from Jenin went to assess the damage and clean up what they could. The checkpoint was closed, which meant Sameer couldn't get across to Jenin. "It was a complete mess," Sameer said. Props and computers were destroyed. At the entrance, the poster for their latest feminist theatre production had been graffitied with a Star of David, as had the white screen in the cinema room.

"It was a very heavy day, to put it lightly," Sameer said. "We started to think what we can do? We quickly realised that our students also need to speak out."

The theatre students, aged between 19 and 25, have been impacted greatly by the arrests. Sameer went back and forth with associate artistic director Zoe Lafferty, and they struck on the idea of starting a series of written testimony. The project is called Youth Against Invasion. Sameer and Lafferty asked the students to write a short piece of text each, then they worked collaboratively on edits. "It's part of how to narrate your own story in your own words."

The stories do not shy away from how the young actors have been impacted by occupation, war and the raid on Jenin. Some of the reading is uncomfortable. For the Freedom Theatre it is part of their cultural resistance: the pieces have been published on social media and read at protests. Two of the pieces are printed below. In the long term, they might become artefacts that reflect the mood and experiences of young artists in Palestine who are so often denied a voice.

Jenin is a place often considered the capital of Palestinian resistance and militancy, and the company is no stranger to conflict. The theatre was officially formed in 2006 by Palestinian-Israeli actor Juliano Mer-Khamis, Swedish activist Jonatan Stanczak and former al Aqsa Martyrs' Brigades leader Zakaria Zubeidi. The story starts slightly before however, when Mer-Khamis' Israeli mother, the human rights activist Arna Mer-Khamis formed The Stone Theatre in 1987 with a vision to work with Palestinians to end the Israeli occupation — a vision the Freedom Theatre has upheld. The Stone Theatre was bulldozed in 2002 by Israeli forces. Juliano Mer-Khamis' documentary Arna's Children tells his mother's story.

Famously, Mer-Khamis told the world: "The third intifada will be a cultural one". In 2011, he was shot dead outside the theatre. The killer was never identified.

As for Zubeidi, he has been held in an Israeli prison since 2019.

"Sometimes we have limitations of course," Sameer began, but when asked for an example of limitations on the company's freedom she paused. "Now you're asking and I'm thinking, 'We talked about that… we talked about everything basically.' But the thing is, you can't go to the next level of talking about it."

One limitation might be nudity

FREEDOM UNDER SIEGE

By YAHYA MAREI

AMONG ALL THE previous raids, this raid was the hardest, because the leaders of Freedom, those who taught me what freedom means, were imprisoned. Despite the pressure we are going through, the phrase 'freedom under siege' came to mind.

I recall what Ahmad Tobasi said, quoting Juliano Mer-Khamis, "The theatre is my AK47".

With all this internal struggle and feelings of revenge, a sense of strength emerges, the strength of the theatre.

Suddenly, an armed Israeli force storms right next to my house, arresting a group of young men and women, my neighbours.

As I look out the window, a mix of emotions floods over me. Looking at my family, I feel fear. Looking at the soldiers, I feel strength and the will to resist. A Zionist commander calls to me, issuing a threat, "You're causing a lot of trouble. Watch out for yourself."

Meanwhile, amidst the gunfire, the local news network composed of mothers reports: "The Freedom Theatre has been raided, its property completely destroyed."

I remember one of the plays that required an actor to portray an Israeli soldier... Now, the real soldier is in the theatre, and the actor, Jamal Abu Joas, is imprisoned.

The occupying forces are trying to suppress all cultural and historical landmarks in Jenin, raiding theatres and demolishing our important landmarks.

I call upon the entire world to take to the streets, wear Palestinian attire, and sing Palestinian songs.

I call on you, to express our culture worldwide.

on stage, but Sameer said that's not something they want to do anyway. Instead, they'll find a different way of performing a scene that doesn't put anyone in danger.

"As a place that's in the middle of Jenin refugee camp, we are part of the community, we are part of whatever is happening in the country, and we respect it," she said, adding that they try to foster respect for ideas.

Outside their work at the theatre, varying degrees of censorship are felt acutely by the theatre's staff and actors when speaking about the ongoing war.

"For each one of us coming from a different area, there's different limitations," Sameer explained. "For instance, me from Jerusalem, I have a different limitation in the freedom of speech and what I can say, and what is censored and what is not censored, than someone coming from Jenin, [or] than a Palestinian living in the Netherlands or wherever."

Sameer added that censorship comes from the Israeli government, as well as places including the USA and EU.

"It is harder for us because we are living immediately under the occupation, because you could lose your job if you talk, because you support what they call terrorism," she said, describing how any cultural resistance can be called terrorism because it is "expressing and exposing the amount of oppression, injustice and brutality".

She told Index she has friends who were arrested for liking social media posts and others who have been beaten after checkpoint soldiers looked through their Instagram feeds. One, she said, was beaten by Israeli soldiers for not having Instagram on their phone at all, with the assumption they must have deleted the app to hide something.

Even before 7 October, running a theatre school in the West Bank was completely different from anywhere else. The simple act of travelling to class, through a checkpoint, starts with the thought: "Maybe I won't arrive". And unlike communities not under occupation, the topics they tackle at the Freedom Theatre are always about resistance. Sameer recalls her own time rehearsing a play at the Freedom Theatre several years ago.

> One play required an actor to portray an Israeli soldier... Now, the real soldier is in the theatre, and the actor is imprisoned

→ "Every night there was an invasion. I remember some days I did not sleep for five minutes," she said. The next morning, they would rehearse, before pausing to grieve, then coming back together to sit and vent. Rehearsals would continue. "Is that normal? I'm completely sure that's not normal. Does that happen elsewhere?"

It was an exhausting way to live and work, but she said: "That gives you the whole energy of continuing. That's why we do this. And that's why we shouldn't stop. Because they want us to stop."

Destruction surrounds the theatre now, which makes accessing it difficult. But the stage is filled with activity and students occupy the space.

"We still go there, we still do classes there, we still meet there," Sameer said. "Because we think it's important to stay, and to be there. And to continue no matter what happens."

Katie Dancey-Downs is assistant editor at Index

WATCHING ANNIHILATION

By **BAHAA ELDIN IBDAH**

SINCE I'M A Palestinian from land taken in 1948, I live and work amongst Israelis. This is the reality I was born into; an Israeli entity, government and state.

In light of the war, as a Palestinian with Israeli citizenship, I cannot do anything. Anyone calling for its end is accused of supporting terrorism. If I post on social media, I will be arrested. If I march in protest, I will be arrested. If I go to pray, I will be assaulted or arrested…

So I have become just a viewer, watching the news and images of the annihilation of my people. As the lives of children, women and the elderly are taken, I have become ashamed and disgraced as a human being - feelings that come before being a Palestinian.

The Israeli occupation has annihilated an entire people. Not only shedding blood, but wiping out thought, laughter, safety and freedom. I cannot express my overwhelming anger, and the only reaction I am allowed is silence. As I watch the desecration and violation of holy places, I remain silent to the point I feel ashamed before God our Creator.

As a Muslim from 48, I have become afraid of publishing Qur'anic verses calling for love and humanity and praying for our innocent martyrs. Even if I go to Al-Aqsa Mosque, there is a checkpoint with occupation forces at the gates.

When I decided to become an actor I was interested in history, culture, politics… But inside 48, I do not feel patriotism or belonging to Palestine. How can I express myself when our freedom has so many limits? When I cannot use my Arabic language first?

So I choose The Freedom Theatre in Jenin Refugee Camp, and to live the life of a Palestinian who directly faces the violence of the occupation forces. An oppression that is not hidden. Where we are not divided. A pure real Palestinian feeling.

Because of The Freedom Theatre, I saw the apartheid wall for the first time and experienced the checkpoints… I saw the life and alleyways of Jenin Camp… The tired walls riddled with bullets. I saw with my naked eyes everything the Israeli army does with all brutality and barbarism. And it increased my belonging.

The repeated aggression on The Freedom Theatre aims to disrupt art and entertainment… To erase our culture and take away a safe space for our skills and dreams. I always feel anxious and afraid. But despite this, we will continue to nurture ourselves so that we can flourish in the gardens…

Our civilisation.

Oh world, do not extinguish the sunlight from our flowers… let them grow and grow. ✖

This piece, alongside the one on p.107, were written by students with Freedom Theatre and Artists on the Frontline, republished here with permission

'Paul Caruana Galizia has given his mother a new and even more lasting monument: a book that is unforgettable, beautifully written, and deeply honest'

John Simpson, THE GUARDIAN

'An unforgettable profile in courage. Riveting and inspiring'
Bill Browder

'Essential reading'
Anne Applebaum

'A murdered mother's fight for truth and justice lives on in the words of her youngest son'
Angelina Jolie

'Devastatingly compelling'
Oliver Balch, FINANCIAL TIMES

'A moving testament to the life and work of an extraordinary woman and the country-changing power of journalism'
Christina Patterson, THE SUNDAY TIMES

'A must-read for anyone who wants to understand what it takes to be an iconoclast and a trailblazer'
Sally Hayden, THE IRISH TIMES

'An eye opener'
NEW YORK TIMES

A Death in Malta
An assassination and a family's quest for justice

PAUL CARUANA GALIZIA

OUT NOW

Fight for life – and language

Amid the Chinese government's ongoing crackdown on Uyghurs in Xinjiang, some members of the diaspora community have launched a campaign to preserve the Uyghur language through children's books. **WILLIAM YANG** talks to them

FOR PROMINENT UYGHUR writer and linguist Abduweli Ayup, the last few years have been overshadowed by tragic news coming out of Xinjiang. In June 2021, he learned about his niece Mihray Erkin's death at a detention centre in the area that is currently part of China. Last May, he found out other family members and friends have been given lengthy sentences.

"I used to try hard to save people from being detained in Xinjiang, but I realised I couldn't save anyone in the end," he told Index in Bergen, Oslo, where he lives in exile with his family. While he continues to advocate on behalf of Uyghurs who are given lengthy sentences, arrested or deported back to China, Ayup has also started a new project: preserving the Uyghur language and culture abroad through the creation and dissemination of books for kids.

"This is a solution of last resort for the Uyghurs because if we don't focus on the Uyghur people in front of us, we will also lose them eventually," he said.

He's part of a network of overseas Uyghurs who have established Uyghur language schools and began to publish Uyghur textbooks for children.

"[In the beginning] we had a group of volunteers, and we talked about having schools and classes," Ayup said. "But the problem is we don't have textbooks, so I began to publish several Uyghur textbooks for children."

After publishing two Uyghur textbooks before the pandemic, Ayup visited some Uyghur schools in Europe and the USA and saw that he needed to modify the content of the books to let them match the language level of most overseas Uyghur children.

"I realised that the text in the books is too complicated for Uyghur children, so I decided to roll out a new series of textbooks," he said, adding that the new books are mostly made up of Uyghur poems, which make it easier for children to learn the language.

"The latest textbook was published in February 2022, and the schools told me the content is much easier for Uyghur children," Ayup added. "I designed images for every vocabulary and hired musicians to write songs for the poems."

While he has been the driving force behind the Uyghur diaspora community's efforts to preserve the language, Ayup said he couldn't have published the textbooks without support and efforts from the community. In addition to funding from diaspora organisations, Uyghur parents play a pivotal role in the efforts to pass the language down to second or third generation overseas Uyghurs.

"Some Uyghur parents in the US drive two hours to send their children to Uyghur schools, and other Uyghur parents try to ensure that Uyghur is the only language spoken in their households," Ayup explained. "We have third-generation Uyghurs in the US and Norway who still keep speaking the Uyghur language."

LEFT: Abduweli Ayup holds up one of his books aimed at children, which is part of his campaign to ensure the Uyghur language remains in use

Since conversations about China's crackdown on the Uyghurs have grown in the last few years, Ayup said some second-generation Uyghurs in their 20s also saw the need to learn the language.

"Conversations about China's persecution of the Uyghurs make these kids realise they are Uyghurs and they should learn the language," he said.

Ayup reckons that while overseas Uyghur children generally don't use Uyghur in their everyday lives, many are actively seeking opportunities to use the language.

"They want to show that they are Uyghur whenever an opportunity arises, so we need to create these opportunities for them," he said.

Over the last decade, the Chinese government has launched a large-scale crackdown on millions of Uyghur Muslims and other Turkic ethnic minorities in its Northwestern Xinjiang Autonomous Region. Since 2017, Chinese authorities have subjected Uyghurs and other ethnic minorities to forced labour programmes, which they've euphemistically labelled "re-education". China's systematic persecution of the Uyghurs has been characterised as "crimes against humanity" by human rights organisations and the UN, while the US State Department said the years-long crackdown on the Uyghurs

> I used to try hard to save people from being detained in Xinjiang, but I realised I couldn't save anyone in the end

ABOVE: Uyghur men in front of a new shop sign featuring large Chinese characters and smaller Uyghur lettering in Xinjiang

constitutes a "genocide".

Amid the Chinese government's campaign to assimilate the Uyghurs, some Uyghur intellectuals say Beijing is trying to completely erase the Uyghur language and culture.

Aziz Isa Elkun, a Uyghur poet based in the UK, told Index: "The Chinese government is forcibly assimilating the Uyghurs into the majority Han Chinese culture through measures such as changing the names of popular Uyghur publications into Chinese terms, enforcing the ban on using Uyghur at school and forcing Uyghurs to adopt Chinese cultural practices."

He said the Chinese government's cultural assimilation campaign against the Uyghurs has caused many Uyghur children in Xinjiang, which the Uyghurs consider their homeland and call East Turkistan, to lose the ability to read and write the Uyghur language. "Under the Chinese Communist Party's rule, the survival of the Uyghur language and culture is at stake," Elkun said.

Apart from concerns expressed by the Uyghur community, a group of independent UN experts also pointed to China's state-run boarding school system in Xinjiang as one of the means for the Chinese government to suppress the use of the Uyghur language.

"Uyghur and other minority children in highly regulated and controlled boarding institutions may have little interaction with their parents, extended family or communities for much of their youth," the experts wrote in a statement released last September, adding that the forced separation of Uyghur children may result in undermining their ties to "their cultural, religious and linguistic identities."

With schools in Xinjiang strictly prohibiting the use of Uyghur language throughout, Ayup and other overseas Uyghurs said the responsibility of preserving the language now rests on the diaspora community.

"Without our efforts, we won't be able to see or hear the Uyghur language anymore," Ayup added.

A Uyghur man named Mahir, who didn't want his full name to be used, and is also based in Norway, told Index: "When I talked to my brother in Xinjiang through video calls, I saw his children only speak Mandarin at home, which was shocking to me."

The mission for Ayup is bringing hope to members of the Uyghur diaspora community. "My theory is that if we can't save Uyghurs who are still in Xinjiang, we should focus on preserving the language and culture abroad." he said. "The most important thing for the diaspora community is hope, and I'm trying to encourage overseas Uyghurs to have hope." ✖

William Yang is a freelance journalist based in Taiwan

LAST WORD

Freedom is very fragile

Ukrainian human rights body the Center for Civil Liberties jointly won the 2022 Nobel Peace Prize. Its head **OLEKSANDRA MATVIICHUK** speaks to Index's **MARK FRARY**

ON 10 DECEMBER 2022, Ukrainian human rights defender Oleksandra Matviichuk stood up in Oslo City Hall in Norway to give an impassioned speech, telling the audience about how peace, progress and human rights are inextricably linked. Matviichuk was accepting the 2022 Nobel Peace Prize on behalf of the Ukrainian human rights organisation Center for Civil Liberties, which she currently heads.

Speaking to Index, she said that the current generation are starting to take democracy for granted. "They have become consumers of values. They perceive freedom as a possibility to choose between cheeses in the supermarket. Therefore, they are ready to exchange freedom for economic benefits, promises of security, or personal comfort. Yet, the truth is that freedom is very fragile."

MF How did you get into human rights activism?

OM In high school, I had the privilege of meeting Yevhen Sverstiuk, a philosopher, writer and former political prisoner of the Soviet Gulag who headed PEN Ukraine. Under his mentorship, I was introduced to the circle of Ukrainian dissidents, individuals I had only read about in history books. They dared to challenge the totalitarian Soviet regime, enduring years in labour camps, exile and psychiatric institutions. This encounter taught me that even when stripped of everything else, one's voice and convictions remain powerful. I decided to pursue law studies with the intention of defending freedom and human dignity.

MF How did things change after the Russian invasion of Crimea in 2014?

OM This was just after the Revolution of Dignity had ended in Ukraine. Millions of people had bravely stood up against a corrupt authoritarian regime. They took to the streets across the entire country, demanding that the regime continue moving towards Europe. When the authoritarian regime fell, Ukraine got its chance for democratic transformation. And to stop Ukraine's progress towards genuine democracy, Russia invaded. CCL was the first human rights organisation to dispatch mobile teams to document war crimes in Crimea and eastern Ukraine. We began documenting abductions, unlawful detentions, torture, rape and killings of civilians.

MF What practical work have you been doing in Ukraine since Russia's wider invasion of the country?

OM We have faced an unprecedented number of war crimes. We united efforts with dozens of regional organisations and built a national network of documenters throughout the country. Working together, we have recorded more than 64,000 episodes of war crimes. It's just the tip of the iceberg.

MF What help does CCL need from outside Ukraine?

OM All this hell we face is the result of the total impunity which Russia has enjoyed for decades. The Russian military has been committing international crimes in Chechnya, Moldova, Georgia, Mali,

ABOVE: The team behind the Center for Civil Liberties in Ukraine, who document war crimes

Libya and Syria. They have never been punished for it. If we want to prevent wars in the future we have to punish states and their leaders who start such wars in the present. But in the whole history of humankind we have only one such precedent. And we still look at the world through the lens of the Nuremberg Trials…Justice should not depend on how and when the war ends. We cannot wait.

MF If you could take one book to jail with you, what would it be?

OM The only book that truly resonates with me is the work of my friend, Victoria Amelina. Victoria, who was a writer before the war, transformed into a war crimes documenter. She dedicated herself to gathering stories of women during the war – civilians, soldiers and volunteers. Tragically, Victoria was killed in the Russian missile attack in Kramatorsk last summer. Now, her book, containing the stories of Ukrainian women, is set to be published. I genuinely hope that the world will hear and appreciate these stories.

MF What news headline would you most like to read?

OM Putin in The Hague. What sentence awaits him, expert opinions. ✖